GRIMSBY

Making The Town
1800-1914

Grimsby town centre in 1961, showing the heart of the medieval town. St James' Church, the Bull Ring and the Old Market Place are clustered at the bottom of the picture, with Victoria Street (to the left) leading up to the Riverhead (in front of the long white-fronted building on the extreme left). In the distance, shadows of clouds help to mark the grid-iron street layout of Victorian housing. (Courtesy of the Grimsby Telegraph, www.thisisgrimsby.co.uk)

GRIMSBY

Making The Town
1800-1914

Alan Dowling

Phillimore

2007

Published by
PHILLIMORE & CO. LTD
Chichester, West Sussex, England
www.phillimore.co.uk

© Alan Dowling, 2007

ISBN 978-1-86077-463-8

Printed and bound in Great Britain

Contents

Dedicated with love to my parents Ethel and Albert,
my sisters Kathleen, Ada, Eileen and May (Maisie),
and my brothers Harry, Albert and Stanley.

List of Illustrations

Frontispiece: Grimsby town centre, 1961

Foreword and Acknowledgements

This book describes the making of Grimsby during the period 1800-1914. In the years leading up to 1800, Grimsby was little more than a market town and decayed port with a population of about one thousand. By 1914 it rejoiced in the title of the world's premier fishing port and was also a successful commercial port and a flourishing regional service centre. It had also experienced a phenomenal rise in population to become the largest town in Lincolnshire, with more than 74,000 inhabitants. Housing that rapidly increasing population led to a large-scale expansion of the town, which is the overriding theme of this book – how the town spread over the ground and how its fields and marshes were transformed into streets and houses. A preliminary chapter introduces the town's early history and some factors that would influence its later development. The greater part of the book then tells the story of Grimsby's physical expansion during 1800-1914. A final chapter surveys the town in more recent times and draws conclusions from the account of its growth.

While writing the book I have been helped by many people. These include the staff of the Grimsby Central Library's Reference Library (in particular Simon Balderson); John Wilson, the North East Lincolnshire archivist; John Callison, the North East Lincolnshire Council's civic manager; and the *Grimsby Telegraph*. The staff of the National Archives at Kew have been a great help during my extensive researches there. The staff of the Clerk to the Enrolled Freemen were also most obliging when I was researching the freemen's records some time ago (many of these records have been deposited since with the North East Lincolnshire Archives). Janet Wilmott has been most helpful and encouraging in reading and advising on the draft text. Ann, John and Roannah Smyth have been very helpful and supportive. Rex Russell permitted me to use some of his excellent enclosure maps, Edwina Shepherd allowed me to use some of her photographs and the staff of the Grimsby Print and Copy Centre have been their usual obliging selves. I apologise to anyone whom I may have inadvertently omitted to thank here.

Illustrations and maps are included by courtesy of the North East Lincolnshire Council Library Service (2-4, 6-9, 11, 13-18, 20-32, 34, 36, 38, 40-1, 43, 45-9, 53-4, 57-8, 60-1, 64, 67-9, 72-6, 78, 81, 91-2, 94), the *Grimsby Telegraph*, www.thisisgrimsby.co.uk (33, 35, 56, 62, 79, 84-5, 87, 93, 95-7), the North East Lincolnshire Archives (1), the Ordnance Survey (37, 44, 51, 63, 70-1, 82-3), Associated British Ports (86, 88), Edwina Shepherd (42, 77), Rex Russell (5, 12) and J. McCulloch (98). The author has provided the remaining illustrations.

Finally I am grateful to my wife Dorothy, without whose encouragement, support, help and suggestions this book would have been neither started nor completed.

Chapter 1

An Extreme Nooke of the Kingdome

In 1634, Grimsby resident Gervase Holles considered the town to be 'seated in an extreme nooke of the Kingdome'.[1] A romantic account of how it came to be located in this 'extreme nooke' is given in the heroic saga of Havelock the Dane. This tells how Havelock, the infant heir to the Danish throne, was threatened with a murderous death but was saved by a Danish fisherman called Grim, who carried him to safety across the North Sea:

> Till they came to a harbour, and left the ship for the land ... At the time of which I tell you, no one lived there or frequented this harbour. He first raised a house there ... he split the ship into two halves, raised up the two ends and they camped inside. He went fishing, as he knew how, and bought and sold salt until he was well-known and recognised by the country folk. Many joined together with him, taking up their quarters at the harbour and because of his name, which they heard, they called the place Grimsby.[2]

Raised in Grimsby by his rescuer, Havelock subsequently married Goldborough, the beautiful but dispossessed heiress to the English throne. He pursued an heroic career, secured both of their inheritances and they reigned jointly over both Denmark and England, making time between royal duties to produce 15 children.

Such has been the widespread popularity of this entertaining account of the town's foundation that it has been retold in several versions. Although it is a legend or folk tale, historians have remarked on some apparent similarities to the town's early history. Edward Gillett has commented that, 'In all this there seem to be shadows of real history', while S.H. Rigby writes that 'In spirit at least ... the story ... probably reflects something of the true origin of the town'.[3] Such a reflection may be seen in the siting of the town at the edge of the coastal marsh on a spur of land leading to the haven, providing a suitable place for settlement and a convenient landing and trading place at the mouth of the Humber estuary.

The town's Scandinavian origins are borne out by its name. The Old Norse personal name 'Grimr' coupled with the Scandinavian suffix 'by', which signifies a settlement, gives us Grimsby, meaning Grim's place, or, if you prefer, Grim's town. Likewise, many of its old streets feature the Scandinavian word 'gata', meaning 'street', as in Deansgate; which was spelt Danesgate c.1220, suggesting that the street had a strong Danish connection.[4] Grimsby is also mentioned in Nordic sagas in connection with the Danish attack upon York in the year 866 but the sagas were written centuries after the actual event so that date can only be conjectural. Certainly, for many centuries, the local populace had a strong interest in the Havelock legend and the town's Scandinavian origins. These were shown

1   *The 13th-century borough seal illustrating the legend of Grim, who is the large central figure. To the left is the smaller figure of Havelock and to the right is Goldborough, who each have a crown above their heads, signifying their royal status. The lettering around the seal reads 'Sigillum comunitatis Grimebye' ('the seal of the corporation of Grimsby')*

in the town's first seal, made in the 13th century, which depicted Grim, Havelock and Goldborough. Also, when the local Wellow Abbey was founded its dedication was to St Olaf, King of Norway, as well as to St Augustine. Even as late as 1791 when John Byng, later Lord Torrington, was being shown around the town's St James' Church, 'The clerk made us observe a very ancient recumbent figure, which he said was of one Grime, who found out this habitation.' This would be the tomb of Sir Thomas Haslerton, which a directory of 1913 noted 'is commonly known as Grim's tomb'.[5]

Undoubtedly, the legendary Grim would have been astonished to learn how much his settlement would expand, until by 2001 his house had been joined by over 36,000 others, in which lived a population of over eighty-seven thousand. Most of this great surge of urban growth occurred in the later 19th and early 20th centuries and was due to the rise and prosperity of the town's industry. It was also dependent on the town's large landowners, who made growth possible by turning their land over to housing. Three of them were particularly important: the municipal corporation, the enrolled freemen and the 1st Lord Heneage. How they developed their land was driven largely by their personalities and motives, which will be examined in detail in an attempt to understand why different areas of the town have exhibited such diverse characteristics. Accordingly, this book has two inter-related themes: firstly, the physical growth of Grimsby and, secondly, the part played in this by its major landowners. Before we begin the story, this chapter will provide an overview of the earlier history of the town and of some of the factors that were to have a bearing on its later expansion.

Domesday Book and Beyond

Archaeological evidence points to land in the area being farmed around 4,000 B.C., with the probability of a trading settlement in the vicinity of Grimsby during the first century B.C. But, moving on from the very early history of the town and its Scandinavian heritage, we come to the account of Grimsby in William the Conqueror's Domesday Book of 1086. From this we see that it had arable and grazing land, a mill and two ferries. In all likelihood it had a church but the Domesday Book entry is not clear on this point. The pre-Norman owners of the town's land had been dispossessed and it had been divided between three Norman lords, namely Odo the Bishop of Bayeux (half-brother of William the Conqueror), Drew De Beurere and Ralf De Mortemer. Some of the land was farmed directly on behalf of these lords. The local people who were beholden to their land-owning lord lived on the remainder. The total population would be about four hundred people.[6]

Domesday Book gives an impression of Grimsby having an economy based on agriculture but the existence of two ferries suggests it was also a trading community. Indeed, the town was one of the ports upon which a tax on overseas trade was levied in 1204. Grimsby was called to pay £91, which placed it in the middle order of East Coast ports, above Barton-on-Humber (£34) and Immingham (£19) but below Newcastle (£158) and far below the major port of Boston (£781). By 1286, Grimsby was a sizeable town with a population of about two thousand. It had two parish churches (St Mary's and St James'), the Wellow Abbey of Augustinian canons, St Leonard's nunnery, the hermitage of St Andrew, two friaries (the Grey Friars and the Austin Friars) and two hospitals.[7] The town also had a 'common hall', which was replaced with a new Town Hall by 1395. The first recorded indication of planned development in the town was in 1341 when the West Haven was excavated and at the same time building was carried out in an area called 'Newbyggyng' ('new building'), which lay to the west of the present Riverhead on land that, at the time of writing, is used for the bus station.[8]

The earliest-known map of the town dates from about 1600 and shows a road layout surprisingly like that on modern street plans. If, for the sake of explanation, we use some modern names, it shows the main route into the town, Bargate, coming in from the south with Abbey Road and Brighowgate branching off to the right. Nearer the built-up area, Cartergate branches off to the left and the main road continues as Deansgate, leading into what is now known as 'Top Town'. This was the medieval heart of the town, which clustered between St James' Church and the Riverhead with outlying building running along Wellowgate and Brighowgate. The lines of other streets such as Victoria Street West and Bethlehem Street can be picked out on the map. We can also see some streets, such

2   *Windmill in the Cartergate area, possibly c.1860, with St James' Church in the background.*

as Flottergate, which have disappeared in recent times under redevelopment schemes. In order to construct and maintain this medieval town, it had bricklayers, carpenters, masons, slaters, thatchers and tilers. Important buildings would incorporate masonry, while bricks were being used in the town as early as the 14th century. However, most houses would have been built of wood with infilling (known in Lincolnshire as 'mud and stud') and with thatched roofs.[9]

Borough and Freemen

A notable occurrence for the town was its advancement to borough status. Grimsby was not listed as a borough in Domesday Book but by 1162 it was being cited as a borough. When Pontefract was granted 'borough liberties' in 1194, these were based on those already being enjoyed by Grimsby. The significance of boroughs was that they were freed from many of the restraints and controls of the existing feudal system and were granted certain freedoms and privileges, which were referred to as 'borough liberties'. Grimsby's liberties were confirmed and amended in several royal charters during succeeding centuries, the first of these being in 1201. The liberties included: the right to hold a borough court; a good degree of self-government; legal, trading and financial privileges; the right to hold fairs and markets and freedom from certain tolls. The borough was also permitted to have two members of parliament from at least as early as 1283.[10]

One effect of being a borough was that it led to the creation of a group of residents known as burgesses or freemen. Although both terms have been used locally, for the sake of clarity they will be referred to as freemen in this book. The basic qualifications for applying to be a freeman in these early days were to be resident in the borough, pay local taxes (known as 'scot and lot') and hold a plot of land in the borough (a 'burgage plot') for which an annual rent was payable to the landowning lord. The number of freemen fluctuated. In the year 1450-1 there were 70 in the town, which may have been about a quarter of the adult male population.[11]

Being a freeman carried both privileges and responsibilities. Economic privileges included preferential treatment when trading in the borough and protection from competition by outsiders. Freemen were also engaged in running the town because of their involvement in the borough court. The court had both judicial and administrative functions and was central to the working of the borough. The officers of the court were the mayor, two bailiffs, two chamberlains, two coroners and other functionaries. The freemen elected these officers from among themselves. Non-freemen did not have the vote and could not hold borough office. Consequently, it was the freemen only who were responsible for the day-to-day operation of the town's judicial and administrative systems.[12]

Most of the court's judicial business was with minor offences, including debt, theft, assault and cases of public nuisance such as blocking sewers, taking stone from road surfaces or depositing dung on the streets.[13] Cases of assault were frequently settled with a fine but theft could be dealt with more harshly. In 1650, 'Ed. Wells, sen., being formally found guiltie of stealinge 1 sheepe ... is adjudged to be stript from the wayst upward and whippt in the [Town] Hall till blood come'. There was no sexual discrimination in dispensing rough justice and in 1692, 'Bridgett, wife of Henry Deane, found guilty of stealing a petticoat, and sentenced to be whipped at the whipping post, stripped to the waist, till her body be bloody.' The court also provided such local government as the town might need and expect. A separate body that evolved from the court later carried out local government. In 1422 this separate body took the form of a mayor's council of 12 freemen, known as 'common councilmen', to which were later added 12 more freemen who had the senior status of aldermen.[14] The mayor's council developed into the borough council, or municipal corporation, which played a major role in the later development of the town.

Town Economy

During the centuries following the Norman Conquest, Grimsby's economy had five major strands to it: overseas trade; coastal trade; fishing; acting as a marketing and service centre and agriculture – all of which were subject to change and fluctuation. Early Scandinavian contacts produced trade in timber, oil, wheat and furs but this trade declined. Trading with the Low Countries became more important, carrying such cargoes as grain, ale, malt, peas, beans and wheat. As the centuries passed Grimsby could not compete in overseas trade with big international ports such as Hull and Boston. Consequently, its coastal trade became more important. Grimsby was one of the main outlets for the grain crops of north Lincolnshire, shipping grain to northern England and Scotland. Coal was the main return cargo from Newcastle and was then traded locally or shipped onwards. Trade was carried on with ports on the Humber and the East Coast, while London was an important destination with its continual demand for foodstuffs.[15]

Fish played a significant part in the town's prosperity up to the 16th century. The herring trade was particularly important and Grimsby boats were also involved in cod fishing off Iceland. Grimsby cod was known in the 13th century when a list of towns and their products referred to the 'Cod of Grimsby'. Fishing also took place with nets that were permanently attached to stakes in the Humber. However, local fishermen did not catch much of the fish that was landed and the town was probably more important as a trading centre in fish rather than in catching the product, which reflects the situation in the port at the time of writing. Local merchants dealt in salmon, turbot, ling, cod, skate and herring. Outsiders came to buy fish and much of the Grimsby fish seems to have gone to towns and villages in northern Lincolnshire and Yorkshire. The fish trade also stimulated the trade in salt, which was used to preserve fish. There was a significant salt-producing industry on the Lincolnshire coast south of Grimsby until the 16th century. Domesday Book credits nearby Tetney with 13 saltpans.[16]

Grimsby also acted as a market town and service centre for its rural hinterland. A large number of residents pursued occupations that were needed to provide basic clothing, food and shelter to the town and its region. We have already noted its building tradesmen. Clothing trades were represented by drapers, fullers, weavers, shearers, dyers, mercers, tailors, tanners, cobblers and glovers. Food and drink purveyors included fishmongers, butchers, bakers and brewers. Other residents were employed as tavern keepers, smiths and mariners while some were involved in boat building and repair. Women's occupations included brewers, bakers and victuallers.[17]

The borough's extensive fields and pastures provided land for arable cultivation and animal husbandry. The town had three large open cornfields that lay to the south of the town astride the present Laceby, Scartho and Weelsby Roads. When the grain harvest was over, all land in the open fields would be thrown open for common grazing by the townspeople's livestock. Other important areas of agricultural land were the Little Field and the Haycroft, in the vicinity of the appropriately named Littlefield Lane and Haycroft Street.[18]

In addition, there were large areas of permanent pasture in the north of the borough known as the East Marsh and the West Marsh. These had originally been salt marsh and in 1341 were granted to the borough by Edward III. The marsh comprised about 120 acres in the 14th century but had increased to 427 acres by 1606 because of natural accretion due to the action of the sea.[19] In about the year 1514, the freemen, in their capacity as the corporation, divided the West Marsh into plots that were leased out for grazing. Most of the plots were reserved for aldermen and councilmen but in 1783 the system was reformed and the plots became available for leasing by the freemen generally, but still not by non-freemen. Another area of corporation land, the East End Closes (in the area of the present Doughty Road), also came to be divided and leased in the same manner.[20]

In contrast to the West Marsh and the East End Closes, the East Marsh was not divided but remained as common pasture, upon which the borough officers and other freemen had greater grazing rights than the non-freemen. Towards the end of the 16th century the mayor could graze 60 sheep, four beasts and a horse on the commons; each alderman 40 sheep and four beasts; each councilman 30 sheep and three beasts; each freeman 20 sheep and two beasts and each non-freeman five sheep and one beast.[21] During the course of succeeding centuries, as other sectors of the town's economy declined, agriculture became more important to the community. Accordingly, land became the source of disputes between the freemen and other residents as the freemen reserved more of the common land to their own use.

A Declining Town

These strands of the town's economy were practised over the centuries largely in the context of a declining town. The growth and prosperity that Grimsby experienced in the two centuries following the Norman Conquest came to an end and complaints of declining prosperity were made by the freemen in 1255, 1280 and 1329; by 1377 the population had fallen to about one thousand five hundred. Long-term urban decline was widespread in the county. Other towns that were affected included Lincoln and Barton-on-Humber.[22] In Grimsby, blame was laid in particular on the condition of the haven, which had played an essential part in the town's foundation and growth but which was subject to severe silting. The haven followed the line of the present Alexandra Dock to the Riverhead and then down what are now New Street, Doughty Road and beyond. It was in an effort to attract trade that the West Haven was excavated in 1341.

The borough also complained that the town's prosperity was affected by competition from markets held in nearby villages and from the new port of Ravenserodd. The latter had begun to develop in the 1230s on an island off the Yorkshire coast near the mouth of the Humber. Even so, Grimsby experienced a spell of increased trade and prosperity in the later 1300s. Local factors producing this could have been the building of the West Haven and the complete destruction of Ravenserodd by floods in 1367.[23] The prosperity was short lived and complaints were made in the following century that in the town 'all is now decayde and waysted' and that the haven was 'wrekyd and stopped'. There was certainly a general decline in the East Coast herring trade, which was not helped by the rise of the Dutch fishing industry. This, plus the continued deterioration of the haven, could have intensified the decline in the town's fish trade. The trade in corn and coal continued but during 1571-2 only 12 vessels used the haven.[24]

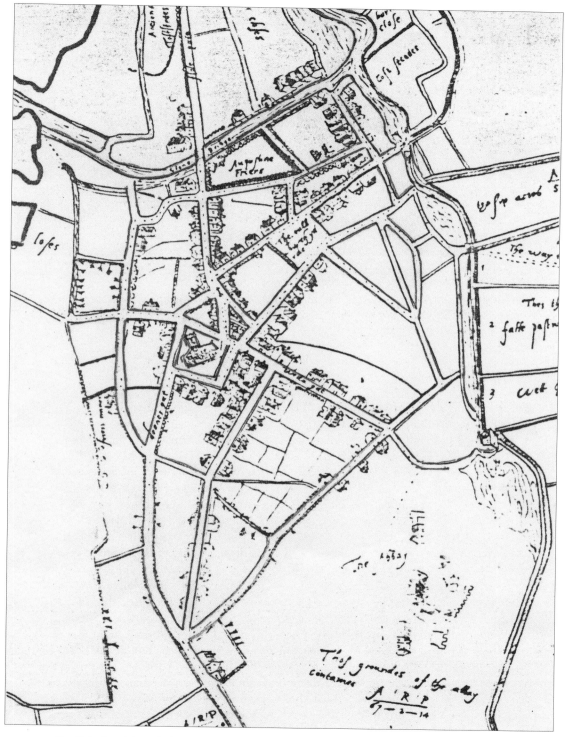

3   *Grimsby c.1600. The lower part of the map shows Bargate coming from the south. Abbey Road and Brighowgate branch off to the right and then Cartergate to the left. The central portion shows St James' Church and the triangular Bull Ring. In the top right-hand quadrant lies the Haven and the West Haven.*

4   *Vicar's tithe barn, which stood in the Bull Ring but fell into disuse after the Enclosure Award of 1840. It is photographed here before the end of 1868.*

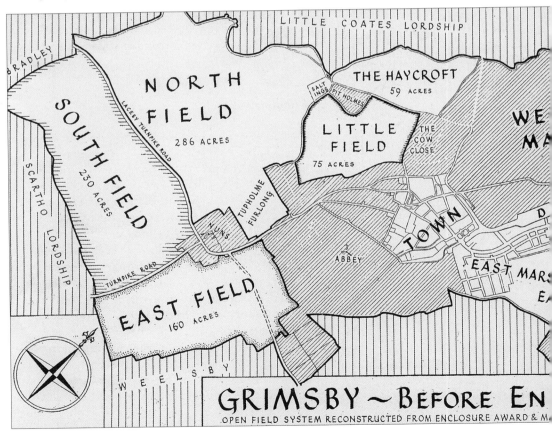

5   *Grimsby's ancient open-field system before the changes wrought by the enclosure of 1827-40.*

The town experienced other major changes in the 16th century, arising from Henry VIII's countrywide dissolution of the monasteries. As a result, the town lost its abbey, nunnery and friaries during the 1530s and the population of the town had fallen to about six hundred in 1563. Symptomatic of the declining population was the redundancy of St Mary's Church. Comment was made in 1533 that the town was 'in great ruin and decay and nothing so populous as it hath been' and did not need two churches. St Mary's Church was demolished by the end of the century. Its site is now the rectangle bounded by East, West and South St Mary's Gate and the stretch of Victoria Street West, which in former times was known as North St Mary's Gate.[25]

Despite the town's decline, freeman, antiquarian, Royalist colonel, Member of Parliament and three-times mayor Gervase Holles (1607-75), who started off our story, acted confidently in 1630. Newly married and having 'money in my purse and contentment in my bed', he made extensive alterations and additions to his house in Grimsby, which was reputedly a stone house on the west side of Haven Street. The house included 'a turret or prospect' from which he could see 'all ships as they sayle the river of Humber'.[26] However, he later gave a gloomy picture of the town when he wrote that, 'the Haven hath been heretofore commodious, now decayed, the traffic good, now gone, the place rich and populous, the houses now mean and straggling by reason of depopulation'.[27]

The beginning of the next century saw a glimmer of hope as action was taken on the haven problem. In the year 1700 work was underway to divert the River Freshney into the haven in order to scour it of mud. Unfortunately, it soon became clear that the scheme was unsuccessful and the haven was once more becoming 'stranded, silted and choked up'.[28]

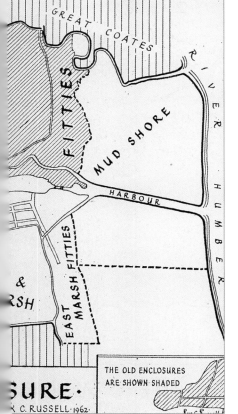

A Middling Village

So, by the beginning of the 1700s, the story of Grimsby during the preceding centuries had been strewn with talk of decline and poverty. Although there was undoubted substance in this, the persistent comparisons of the current state of Grimsby with what it had been in some halcyon distant past give an impression of a town with more than its fair share of obsessive doom and gloom. Even visiting clergyman Abraham de la Pryme could not resist pontificating in 1697 that 'Grimsby at present is but a little poor town, not a quarter so great as heretofore.' John Wesley joined in the fun on his visit in 1766, writing: 'Grimsby was one of the largest towns in the county; it is now no bigger than a middling village.'[29]

But despite its decline Grimsby was more than Wesley's middling village. It is true that the town's built-up area was comparatively small but it was long established as a local marketing and service centre for its rural hinterland. It is also striking that the borough contained an extensive resource of agricultural land. To the south were the 500 or so acres of the cornfields; to

6   *A sketch of buildings in Grimsby before 1857 by George Skelton, entitled 'Market Place Grimsby. Site of Cornexchange' [sic].*

the west lay the Little Field and the Haycroft and to the north more than 400 acres of pasture in the West and East Marshes. There is little doubt that Grimsby was able to fall back on these economic resources and, despite its decline, survive into the 18th century as a market town and agricultural community. There were also signs of a new positive outlook. Local landowners, farmers and merchants subscribed to obtain a turnpike act in 1765 and new roads were constructed from Grimsby into its rural hinterland, anticipating increased trade with agricultural communities. New warehouses began to be built and, in 1780, a new Town Hall was erected to replace the one built in the 14th century. Also significant was that, after many centuries of decline, the population was at last on the increase, possibly reaching about one thousand persons by mid-century.[30]

Chapter 2

New Dock, New Town

1796-1830s

In the final quarter of the 18th century, Grimsby was effectively a market town that had been obliged to turn its back on its maritime past. However, it retained its ancient privilege of electing two members of parliament, which made it a political cockpit at parliamentary elections. It was political manoeuvrings that were to direct attention once more to the haven and give hope for a more prosperous future.

Politics and the Haven

The borough was divided politically between two factions, known respectively as the 'Blues' (the Whigs) and the 'Reds' (the Tories). The Whigs were headed by Charles Anderson Pelham (1748-1823). He became Lord Yarborough in 1794 when he was ennobled as the 1st Baron Yarborough. His ancestor, Sir William Pelham, one of Elizabeth I's commanders, had settled in the Brocklesby area, about seven miles to the west of Grimsby, in the 16th century. Over time the family acquired vast areas of land by purchase and advantageous marriages until they became the largest landowners in Lincolnshire, holding over 56,000 acres. The Tories were led by prominent attorney and landowner George Tennyson (1750-1835). The Tennyson family, originally from East Yorkshire, had arrived in Grimsby in the early 18th century. They benefited from intermarriage with the Clayton family, who were the borough's most prominent and politically influential family. When the Clayton line died out George Tennyson inherited their wealth and political influence.

Tennyson had land adjacent to the haven. If the latter were improved, it would not only benefit his land but also give him increased political clout. Accordingly, in 1787, his local agent asked engineer Jonathan Pickernell of Whitby to draw up plans for the haven to be transformed into a dock. The scheme came to the fore in the build-up to the 1796 parliamentary election. The municipal corporation supported the scheme and Yarborough realised that it would be a political mistake to oppose it. Accordingly, a compromise was reached with Tennyson. They would each put forward one candidate only, thus sharing the parliamentary seats, and would also unite behind the haven scheme. Consequently, a parliamentary bill was enacted on 14 May 1796 authorising the formation of the Grimsby Haven Company and the construction of a dock.[1]

The initial share capital of the company was £30,000 but this was increased to £60,000 under a further act in 1799. Most of the capital came from landowners and larger farmers, who together contributed £39,207 or 65 per cent of the authorised capital. Between them

7   *Red Hill on a sunny day in June 1924. It ran between Flottergate and Cartergate. Reputedly named because of its association with the 'Red' (Tory) political faction in the 18th century, it was previously known as Pinfold Hill.*

they owned the bulk of the Lincolnshire Wolds and their interest in Grimsby was linked to the intention to increase the profitability of their land. Their produce could be carried to Grimsby on the turnpike road that ran between Grimsby and the Wolds; many of them were also shareholders in the turnpike trust. In addition, those who owned land in Grimsby expected to benefit from an increased demand for urban land.[2]

The largest shareholder in the haven company, subscribing £4,822, was John Julius Angerstein (1735-1823), London banker, stockbroker and philanthropist who had extensive land holdings in Lincolnshire. Tennyson and Yarborough each held shares to the value of £3,215. The municipal corporation became heavily involved, holding £3,715 in shares. The corporation's involvement was essential to the scheme going forward. Some of its land would be needed for the construction of the dock and for dockside commercial development. It made the land available and took an active part in supporting the venture. The town clerk, George Babb, who had assisted the promoters of the scheme in getting corporation support, became the Grimsby Haven Company's clerk and was chiefly responsible for the organisation (or rather, disorganisation) of the company and its finances. Babb was succeeded on his death in 1824 by his son (also George) as town clerk and clerk to the Haven Company. George the younger (1793-1861) followed in his father's footsteps in muddling the company's finances.[3]

New Dock

Pickernell was appointed company engineer and stated that his plans for the haven would 'Render that Port of very Great Moment'. Well-known agriculturalist Arthur Young commented that 'They have a speculation, if they succeed, of rivalling Hull, as the great entrepôt of the Humber.' However, Pickernell's plans were far more extensive and costly than had been envisaged and brought opposition, especially from Babb the elder, who pressed for the adoption of cheaper schemes. Babb's attitude was symptomatic of the company in general, which underestimated the difficulties of the work and its cost. Pickernell was soon dismissed and work continued without an engineer. After a series of setbacks, the country's leading dock engineer, John Rennie, agreed to take charge of the project in 1798 and set about completing what would be the largest dock in the country at that time. Celebrations to mark the completion of the work were held on 30 December 1800 and the bells of St James' Church rang out in celebration, while local notables sat down to a banquet at the company's expense.[4]

With the opening of the dock to shipping during 1801, Grimsby entered the new century with optimism and high expectations as the long-term problems with the haven appeared to have been solved. In an attempt to revive the fishing industry, the corporation paid a bounty of 10 shillings to the first cobble in any week to land fish, and the following advertisement appeared:

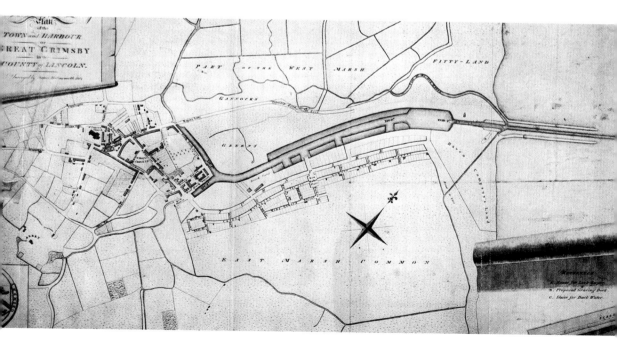

8   *Newly completed Haven Dock, 1801. The old town and the Riverhead and West Haven are to the left. The emerging New Town is set out centrally on the East Marsh Lots to the south of the dock.*

The port of Grimsby being the nearest port to the Dogger Bank in the North Sea, and very convenient for the fishing trade, it is intended this season which commences with Lent to supply this part of the country and neighbouring counties with cod, haddock, ling, butts, skate etcetera, two cobbles being already engaged for that purpose. The advantage arising from the selection of Grimsby is that when the north-west or north-north-west winds prevail, which frequently happens during the fishing months, boats find no difficulty in making this harbour when it is impossible to make any other up the river.[5]

Although the fishing trade showed no great revival, commercial trade improved and ships came to Grimsby from such distant ports as Quebec, Halifax, Rostock, Gallipoli and the Baltic. During 1805, 68 ships brought cargoes of timber, tar, linseed, wheat and whale oil. Unfortunately, the initial impetus was not sustained. A major drawback was the inability to provide ships with return cargoes. In 1807 only 11 ships entered the port and only three left with cargoes. Some whaling was carried on during 1803-6 and staggered on for a few more years.[6] A dry dock was completed in 1804 and joined by another later on but their chief function was ship repair. In the first 13 years of the century only 12 ships were built in Grimsby. Neither overseas nor coastal traffic was very great. The Napoleonic War no doubt affected commerce; trade with the Baltic was interrupted and the price of timber rose tenfold.[7]

With regard to coastal trade, during 1813-32 the largest number of coasters entering the port in a year was 37; during 1844-6 the annual average had fallen to 29 coasters. This compares poorly with Goole, which during 1828-34 annually averaged 1,240 boats entering the port. The Haven Company sought to increase trade by carrying out more improvements to the dock and on 10 June 1825 the third Haven Act became law, which allowed the company to raise a further £10,000. After closure for some improvement work, the dock reopened in 1826. This was followed by an increase in shipping, only to be followed by another decline.[8] Expectations were raised in 1830 when the corporation leased land in the East Marsh Fitties to the borough Member of Parliament, Captain George Harris, for the construction of a ropery and flax mill. It was built along the north side of Cleethorpe Road between what are now Riby Square and Humber Street. Unfortunately, it came to grief after a gale in 1833 when more than half the building was blown down. It never recovered from the disaster.[9]

Despite the over-optimistic and unrealised hopes for the dock, the town did experience some increase in trade and its population rose from 1,524 in 1801 to 4,225 in 1831. However, the subsequent decline led to the population falling to 3,700 in 1841. There were two main reasons for the dock not fulfilling expectations. Firstly, it had no existing community of merchants with the necessary mercantile experience and trading contacts and, secondly, it had no easy communication with a sizeable and varied hinterland that

9   *The Ropery and Ropery Houses, 1847. The Ropery was built in the early 1830s and lay on the north side of Cleethorpe Road between Riby Square and Humber Street.*

would provide a year-round supply of exports and a steady market for imports. These drawbacks were not foreseen when the dock opened and the prospect of flourishing marine, commercial and industrial activity led directly to the physical expansion of the town on to the East Marsh. This process was initiated and carried out by the municipal corporation and the freemen, at whom we must take a close look before describing what happened, and seeing how they created what became known as the 'New Town'.

Corporation and Freemen

The overriding impression of the early 19th century is the privileged position that the freemen held in the town. At that time admission to the borough's roll of freemen (becoming an 'enrolled freeman') was gained either by being born the son of a freeman, by marrying a freeman's daughter or widow, or by apprenticeship to a freeman. The ancient need to hold a burgage plot of land no longer applied and the practice of being able to become a freeman by purchase had died out. The entire body of the town's three hundred or so freemen comprised the municipal corporation and would occasionally meet together in a 'Full Court' when matters crucially important to the town or their own well-being were under discussion. However, the borough council, which was elected by the freemen from among themselves, carried out the day-to-day administration of the borough; non-freemen did not have the municipal vote and could not hold municipal office. The mayor, who was elected annually by the freemen, headed the council. The other members of the council, namely 12 aldermen and 12 councilmen, were elected for life by the freemen, as was the town clerk.

There were 313 freemen in the borough in 1831, which would be about a third of the adult male population. Their economic and social composition covered a wide range. About ten of them could be classed as of professional or similar standing, or were of independent means. The majority, about 218, were in the middle order of occupations such as those connected with trades and services (shopkeepers, tradesmen, craftsmen); or with the port (mariners, harbour master, dock master, ship carpenters, lock-keepers); or farming (there were nine farmers although others grazed stock as a subsidiary activity). However, well over a quarter, 85 in total, were in partly skilled or unskilled occupations. Of these, 56 were labourers, which was the most heavily represented individual occupation.[10]

It was this assorted group that comprised the municipal corporation, which by this time saw its main duty as meeting the interests of its own members, the freemen themselves. Consequently, it is not surprising that the freemen (in their capacity as the corporation) gave themselves many personal benefits. They were given preference when paid work had to be carried out for the corporation and also had free education for their children at the freemen's schools, which were maintained and financed by the corporation. Municipal elections provided opportunities for other benefits, which included a payment of five shillings to each freeman for attending the annual election of the mayor. This was at a time when local labourers' wages ranged from 12 to 18 shillings a week.[11]

Bribery and Corruption

The corporation was a battleground for the two opposing political parties, who were quite happy to bribe the freemen to get their supporters appointed as borough officers. These officers, particularly the mayor, wielded power and influence. It was the mayor who decided who was eligible to vote and, therefore, could rig the ballot in favour of the party he supported. Mayors were elected from the aldermen, so it was important to get men of your own political persuasion into their ranks. This practice was illustrated in a comment from 1834 on an election to appoint a new alderman:

> During the contest, £500 or £600 have [sic] been expended by each party in the election of an alderman. These sums were spent in treating and bribing voters. At present about £50 is [also] expended by every new alderman on his election, of which sum 2s. 6d. is usually given to each freeman, and the rest expended in a dinner.[12]

There was much greater potential for financial benefits at parliamentary elections. As with the municipal elections, only freemen had the vote and, as the secret ballot had not yet been introduced, bribery was widespread. When William Cobbett visited the town in 1830 he called it a sink of corruption.[13] Historian Edward Gillett has commented that, 'To the freemen of Victorian times, the beginning of the 19th century seemed a silver age. The old corporation had never been more deeply sunk in political corruption ... there was bribery at every election'.[14]

Candidates for election would bribe freemen with food, drink, offers of employment and money, so much so that, in 1763, when the Methodist Conference passed a resolution against bribery, it went on to say: 'Let this be particularly observed at Grimsby'.[15] The town's parliamentary election of 1790 was subject to scrutiny by parliament because of accusations of bribery, which may have prompted the remark of John Byng on his visit in 1791 that the town was 'now a wretched borough, existing only by venality'.[16] It was reckoned locally that £20 was 'the usual compliment' for a vote at parliamentary elections and by the 19th century the financial rewards of voting were considered to be the chief reason for becoming a freeman.[17] When George Heneage lost the election in 1830, it was thought that it may have been partly due to his agent, Joseph Daubney, not paying the voters enough and also insulting them by saying, 'Damn them, they may be bought like sheep at Smithfield when they are wanted'.[18]

In addition to the bribery, Grimsby parliamentary elections were rumbustious affairs. Voters of the opposing side could be prevented from voting by various stratagems. Some were kept drunk or forcibly hidden away, either on land or aboard ship, until the voting was over. Other steps could be taken against non-freemen who would have the vote after marriage to a freeman's daughter. Stories tell of them being enticed on to boats and carried out to sea, not being brought back until the election was over, while others tell of their prospective brides being locked away until the voting was finished.[19]

Planning a New Town

Despite the advantages available to freemen at election times, their most significant long-term benefits were those connected with land. We shall now see how these led to the beginning of Grimsby's modern urban development. Firstly, we should note that the use of 99-year building leases became an important factor in the town's development. In 19th-century Grimsby, land for housing was not usually sold freehold but leased out on 99-year building leases. The benefits of such leases to the landowner (the lessor) were that it kept his estate intact, relieved him of the risks of speculative building and gave him a steady income in annual ground rents. It also provided a bonus when the leases expired because the current lessor not only regained the land but also became the owner of any property that had been built on it. A benefit to the leaseholder (the lessee) was that he could obtain building land without a large capital outlay.

So where did the corporation and freemen begin the town's 19th-century leasehold development? It took place on land adjacent to the new dock. The dock was bounded on the east by the corporation's East Marsh open common, of which the freemen had the monopoly of pasturage or other uses. Consequently, both the corporation as a local authority and the freemen as individuals saw possibilities of financial benefits arising from the use of the land for either trading premises or housing. Therefore, the corporation started leasing out land on 99-year building leases in 1800. Two areas of land were put up for leasing. One piece was made available for trade purposes and consisted of approximately 16 acres. It lay between what are now the Alexandra Dock and Victoria Street North and

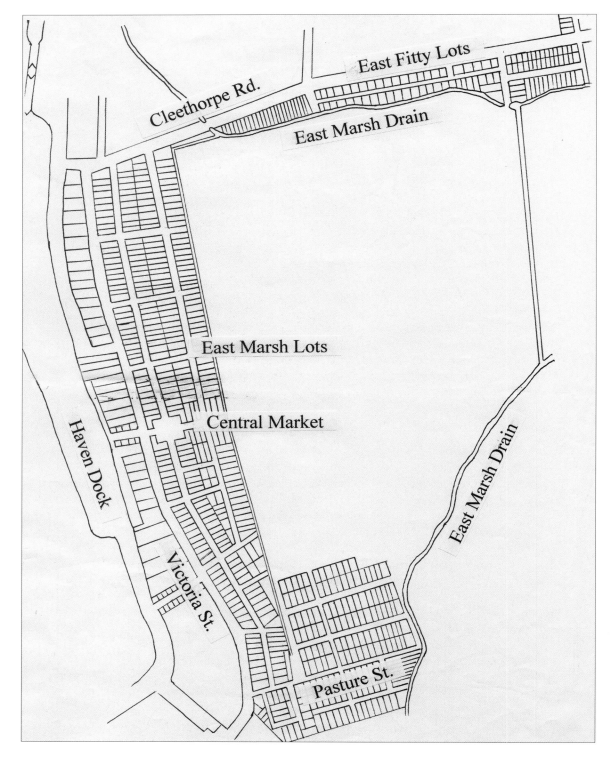

10   *East Marsh Lots (the New Town) and East Fitty Lots, as set out during 1801-32.*

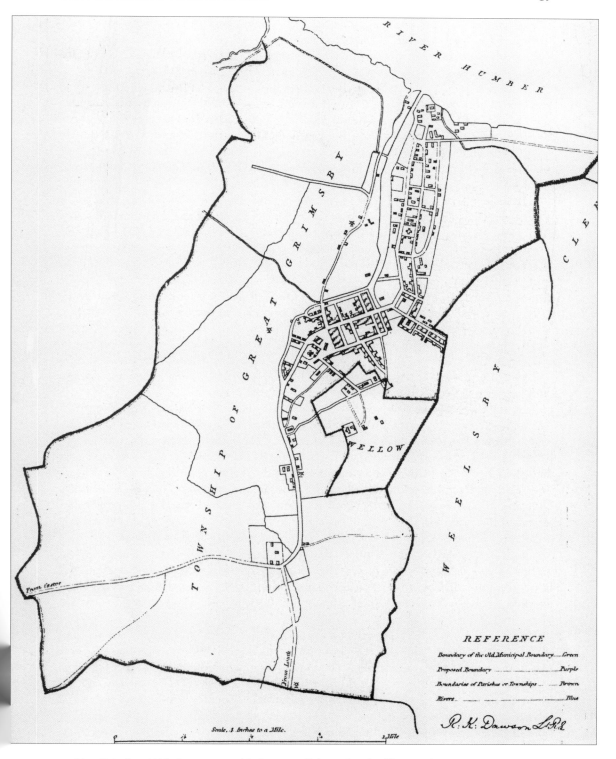

11 *Grimsby c.1830, showing most of the housing still clustered in the old town. The Haven Dock stretches to the north; to its right lies the scattered housing of the East Marsh Lots (the New Town).*

stretched between Ranters' Wharf and Lock Hill. Leasehold plots were offered to freemen 'who are concerned in Trade, as Timber, Coal, Corn, or other Merchandize'. Despite being given preference, the freemen showed muted interest, 32 of the 61 lots having to be put up for auction to the general public.[20]

Of more personal interest to the freemen and more significant in the long term was the second area of land. This was leased out for house building and became known as the East Marsh Lots and the East Fitty Lots. The East Marsh Lots lay between Victoria Street North and the present railway lines and stretched between Pasture Street and Lock Hill. The main streets were Burgess Street and King Edward Street. The East Marsh Lots merged into the East Fitty Lots, which lay further north along Cleethorpe Road, and included the present Strand Street.

The East Marsh Lots and East Fitty Lots were ideally placed to provide a northern extension of the old town and would be handy for the new dock and dockside industries. The corporation's development was set out in an impressive manner and had a clear and logical street plan. The plan included a market place and standard-sized building lots of 360 square yards, each being 12 yards wide by 30 yards deep. The corporation stipulated that houses should be built in a 'workmanlike manner' with one or more brick and tile houses on each lot. It would not permit 'any Trade or Business which may be nauseous ... or grow to the Annoyance or Disturbance of any other Lessees or Tenants'. No stables, slaughterhouses or other nuisances were to be built on the front of any street. Another condition was that the houses should be built within 10 years of the commencement of the leases.[21] We shall see that later in the century each of our landowners used similar conditions or covenants, with the aim of achieving and maintaining a high standard of development. We shall also see whether this aim was realised.

The building lots were allocated by ballot to the freemen only. Each freeman was entitled to one lot. Not every freeman wanted, or could afford, a lot and those lots not taken by freemen were put up for public auction to the highest bidder, whether freeman or not. Initially, 234 lots were set out and allocated in 1800. They were divided into Front Lots and Back Lots. The former were along the east side of Victoria Street North and were leased to the freemen on advantageous terms, i.e. an annual ground rent of 10 shillings plus an initial one-off fee of £12. The Back Lots were in the back and side streets and carried a lower ground rent of 5 shillings plus a fee of £4. The lots were almost entirely taken up, only seven being left not assigned. Further allocations of lots followed in 1803, 1812, 1825 and 1832. Lessees were subsequently allowed to purchase the freehold of their lots but had to continue paying their annual ground rent. This benefited both the lessees and the corporation; the former became the outright owners of their lots while the corporation not only received the purchase price of the lots but also continued to receive the annual ground rents.

To summarise this development, between 1800 and 1832, allocations were made of 456 East Marsh Lots and 117 East Fitty Lots. These amounted to over 45 acres (53 if roads and market place are included). In addition, another 33 acres or so were leased or sold for industrial and trading purposes. Accordingly, during 1800-32 the corporation transferred nearly one hundred acres of the freemen's common pasture to the individual ownership of freemen and others. In 1837 it was estimated that 118 acres of the East Marsh remained as freemen's common pasture.[22]

In contrast to those freemen who did not want lots, some freemen and others wanted larger holdings of land for large-scale use or investment. Lots could be exchanged or sold and additional ones could be acquired at the auctions of those not taken up by freemen.

Town clerk George Babb the younger purchased 11 lots in 1829. William Bennett, wine and spirit merchant, purchased 14 lots in a block in 1835, which later accommodated an ironworks. A notable purchaser of lots was solicitor and land agent Joseph Daubney. He was not a freeman but acquired at least 56 lots; whether he purchased these for himself or as an intermediary for others is not known.[23]

New Town, False Start

Despite being leased for building, many of the lots were not built on and were used for other purposes. When the allocation of lots commenced in 1800, there was no immediate surge of building on the land. In September 1801, there were 'potatoes, cabbages, carrots and turnips, etc., now growing in the greater part of the building lots in the East Marsh'.[24] There is no evidence of a local house-building industry in 1800 that was sufficiently organised and financed to be able to undertake large-scale speculative building with confidence. This, coupled with the multitude of small building lots, meant that house building followed demand on a piecemeal basis. Although building did take place to house the town's increasing population, the rate of development fluctuated with the well-being of the dock trade. By 1808, 'the bottom had dropped out of the property market' and in 1819 the town clerk wrote that 'from the great deficiency in ... Sea Trade ... the New Town is deserting for the Old, by People in Trade'. A resurgence of trade followed the improvements to the dock in the 1820s but more retreat from the new to the old town followed in the 1830s.[25]

Many of the lots continued to be used as gardens for growing vegetables or flowers. Larger areas were being used as paddocks as late as 1845. Other land was described as 'unfenced and uncultivated receptacles for nuisances to the annoyance of occupiers of adjoining Houses'.[26] So, despite the major change in land use that was anticipated by the allocation of the lots, many of them lay bereft of housing. It is also apparent that the corporation's building conditions were largely ignored. There was no apparatus to ensure that lessees complied with the conditions. In effect, they were free to use the land according to their own needs and the needs of others, whether these were for agricultural, commercial or housing purposes. Despite these deficiencies in this early example of town planning, building did take place on the lots and people did live there and pursue trades and businesses. The area achieved its own identity and become known as the New Town.

Chapter 3

Reform and Divide
1827-1840

While the leasing and selling of corporation land was underway in the planning of the New Town, events or reforms were taking place that would have major long-term repercussions on what sort of town would be built in Victorian times.

Land Reform, 1827-40

The first of these events concerned the corporation's agricultural land and the process of parliamentary enclosure. The old-established form of agriculture in most of the county, including Grimsby, was the open-field system, under which farming took place on a communal basis and an owner's land could be scattered in many small plots in several very large fields. Such fragmentation and communal control was not favourable to improved or alternative land use, whether for agriculture, building, commerce or industry. Consequently, larger landowners in a parish could combine to obtain an act of parliament that would enable a process known as parliamentary enclosure (or inclosure) to begin. Under this procedure an enclosure commissioner was appointed, who decided how land should be shared out and also set out new drains, roads and footpaths. Thus a landowner's fragmented land holdings were brought together and enclosed with hedges. The resulting smaller enclosed fields, now with sole and independent owners, were more adaptable for improved farming practices or other uses. This process applied only to the land in the large open fields. Other land, known as old inclosures, was not affected.

The corporation estate before parliamentary enclosure consisted of four major components, namely:

– The land on the East Marsh comprising the New Town (the East Marsh Lots and the East Fitty Lots), which, as we have seen, had been leased or sold to individual freemen and others.

– The remainder of the East Marsh, which was still being used as common grazing for freemen's stock.

– The West Marsh and the East End Closes, which were divided into grazing paddocks and leased to individual freemen.

– The corporation/freemen's rights regarding land in the open fields, particularly in the Little Field and the Haycroft.

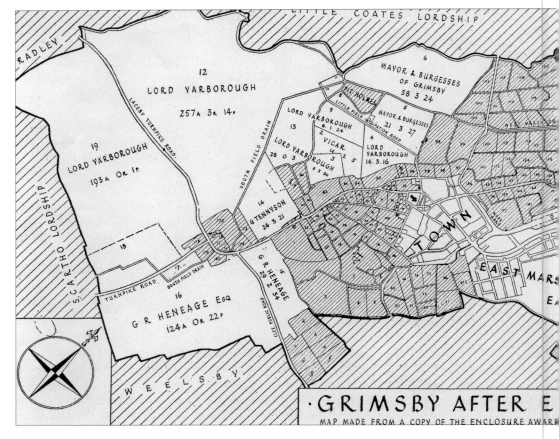

12 *Land ownership after the enclosure of 1827-40.*

Of this large estate, it was the common grazing land in the East Marsh to which attention was drawn in the 1820s. By then, only a small number of freemen benefited from this land because only a minority still grazed stock. An anonymous freeman drew attention to this by way of a public notice[1] in 1824 and suggested how all the freemen might benefit better from their common grazing land:

> At this time, about fifty [freemen] get what belongs to three hundred; whereas the whole of the Land belonging to us might be so enclosed and divided as to afford every Burgess [freeman] some benefit, in one way or other, for if he have not stock, he may receive a yearly Rent.

He then suggested that obtaining an enclosure act and appointing a freeman as the enclosure commissioner would be a way of achieving this. He also urged the need to get the co-operation of the other large landowners:

> An Act, I think, might with little difficulty be obtained ... First call a Full Court, and ... appoint a commissioner from among ourselves, for surely we can find one qualified ... when we consider, a Cock can always fight best on his own midden ... Unite then and do this at the

MUD SHORE

HARBOUR

THE OLD ENCLOSURES
ARE SHOWN SHADED

)SURE·

EX C. RUSSELL 1962

next Court, and try if Lord Yarborough, Mr Heneage, and Messrs. [*sic*] Tennyson, will not meet us.

He then finished on the theme of getting justice and benefit for all the freemen:

> But mind and make a condition, that we shall have the Little Field and Haycroft, or so much of both or either as in Justice, we shall be found entitled to; then we may fix things in such a way, as for all to be benefited alike, and not as now, one part live on the vitals of the other.

In addition to the likelihood of enclosure influencing the freemen's well being, it could also affect the corporation's finances. Most of its income came from its land. In 1827-8, of its total annual income of £1,086, the greater part, £1,002, came from the estate. This income was spent largely by the corporation on maintaining itself, its estate and the freemen's benefits. The town clerk's analysis in 1834 of ordinary annual expenditure of £1,130 revealed that over a third was related to land, including the payment of tithes, nearly a third was related to the freemen's schools and most of the rest was payments to corporation officials (all freemen) and other freemen.[2]

So the question of parliamentary enclosure was important to both the corporation and the individual freemen and, in 1826, 72 freemen signed a requisition to the mayor to call a Full Court to consider enclosure. The court was held but the freemen were divided and a majority voted against.[3] There was uncertainty whether the freemen might lose more than they gained, particularly in the East and West Marshes. However, solicitor Joseph Daubney, presumably at the behest of the major private landowners, set out to force the freemen's hands. Accordingly, on 6 November 1826 he inserted a public notice in the county newspaper stating that application was to be made to parliament for an enclosure act. He then issued a handbill addressed to the freemen apologising for his precipitate action and explaining why it was important to the town to have an enclosure act.[4] It would enable land to be made available to merchants and others and:

> In my judgement, the many Thousand Pounds you have laid out in the improvement of the Town and Haven, the latter of which is now perfect, will be lost, unless you effect an Inclosure – this is the only thing remaining to be done, to enable the place to rival any in the Kingdom in Commercial convenience, Improvement and prosperity.

He also sought to allay the freemen's fears by assuring them that:

> I do not mean an Inclosure that would cut up your East Marsh, or disturb your West Marshes, I would leave you in the perfect enjoyment of them, as they are now; and I would add to the enjoyment of these, another Tract of Land, extending across the Little Field and including the Haycroft.

13   *Bull Ring, south side, 1850, by George Skelton.*

Acting on such assurances that their existing corporation estate would be protected and that they would get extra land in the Haycroft and Little Field, the freemen met in Full Court three months later. Those present agreed by 166 votes to 30 to petition parliament for an enclosure act.[5] Accordingly, acting in co-operation with the major private landowners, application for an act was made to parliament.

The Grimsby enclosure act came into force on 28 May 1827 and an enclosure commissioner was appointed. The freemen did not get their own man into this crucial position. Instead it was given to Lord Yarborough's land steward, John Burcham. The results of Burcham's decisions were set down in what is known as an enclosure award. It did not include all the land in the borough but revealed Lord Yarborough as the largest landowner with at least 692 acres. The corporation was next largest with 538 acres. George Heneage was awarded 160 acres and George Tennyson held at least 32 acres.[6]

It was later asserted that the freemen's consent to enclosure had been achieved by bribery:

> This measure was brought forward ... shortly after an election when the freemen had been paid what is called the usual compliment; viz. £20 for their votes. The freemen appear to have been unfairly dealt with in this business, in not having been informed of the probable effect of the inclosure. The value of the corporation property, however, is estimated to have been increased by the inclosure more than £1,600. The recorder [Lord Yarborough] and other landowners appear to have been materially benefited by it. The commissioner under the Act [John Burcham] was the land steward of the recorder and of another landed proprietor.[7]

The corporation's land in the West Marsh, the East End Closes and the East Marsh was not affected by the enclosure and in addition it now had ownership of 80 acres in the Little

14 *Cottages in front of St. James' Church; by George Skelton. These cottages were criticised as overcrowded and not fit for habitation in 1850. At the same time, the churchyard behind the cottages was noisome and full to overflowing.*

Field and the Haycroft. Although the enclosure award was not formally completed until 1840, the corporation had access to its additional land in the Little Field and the Haycroft by 1829. A decision then had to be made on how this new land should be used, whether as common grazing like the East Marsh or divided into paddocks like the West Marsh and East End Closes. After several lively meetings, the freemen decided that the Little Field and the Haycroft should not be divided into paddocks but used in common by the freemen, like the East Marsh. They also paid attention to the anonymous public notice of 1824 and decided that those freemen who pastured stock on their common land should pay for the privilege, and that the money thus raised should be divided equally among those freemen who did not stock. Thus we see an early indication of the concept of the freemen's annual dividend.[8]

As a result of the freemen's decision on the use of the Little Field and the Haycroft, the corporation land that was still in agricultural use now consisted of two clearly defined categories, as follows:

–   On the one hand was land that was divided into paddocks and leased to a few individual freemen from whom the corporation took rents. This land consisted of the West Marsh and the East End Closes.

–   On the other hand was open land that was available as common grazing for all the freemen. This land consisted of the East Marsh, Little Field and Haycroft. Those freemen who did not graze stock on this land could receive a money payment in lieu.

We shall see that this division of the estate into two categories was to have long-term implications for the corporation, the freemen and the town.

15   *Clayton Hall, Baxtergate [Victoria Street West] c.1820; by George Skelton. The Claytons had been one of Grimsby's foremost families in the previous century.*

Parliamentary Reform, 1832

The next major event for the corporation and freemen was a parliamentary reform bill. As part of its countrywide reforms the bill's proposals would severely curtail the freemen's influence at elections and also reduce Grimsby to a single-member constituency. Accordingly, the corporation and freemen petitioned parliament: 'Your petitioners view with sentiments of regret and deep apprehension the proposed curtailment of their birthright and chartered privileges and humbly pray that your honourable house will discountenance that part of the measure calculated to disfranchise the children and posterity of your petitioners.'[9]

The phrases relating to 'birthright and chartered privileges' and 'the children and posterity of your petitioners' are typical of the language that would be used on occasions during the century when the freemen's privileges were, or were thought to be, under attack. In the event, the petition had no effect and the bill was enacted as the Parliamentary Reform Act of 1832. Under the act, Grimsby was indeed reduced to a single-member constituency as part of a national redistribution of parliamentary seats. Most importantly, the freemen lost their monopoly of the parliamentary vote, which would be held henceforth by occupiers of premises worth £10 in annual rent, whether freemen or not. Those who were already freemen kept the vote but the act ensured that no new freemen would get the vote just because they were freemen. In addition, the constituency was extended to take in adjacent villages and Cleethorpes. The outcome of these measures was to lessen the freemen's influence at election times and decrease the opportunities for bribery. The immediate effect was to reduce the freemen's vote to 61 per cent of the electorate in the enlarged constituency, instead of the monopoly which they had held hitherto.[10] This percentage would decline over the century.

Municipal Reform, 1835

An even more significant event was the passing of the Municipal Reform Act of 1835, which was designed to sweep away such inadequate and corrupt borough corporations as Grimsby, aptly called 'snug oases of privilege'. They were replaced with reformed corporations that, henceforth, were subject to a degree of regulation by central government, particularly the Treasury.[11] Under the act, the freemen lost their monopoly of municipal office, while the old corporation's elected-for-life aldermen and councilmen were replaced by four aldermen and 12 councillors who were subject to regular re-election. The freemen's monopoly of the municipal vote was also broken, it being extended to all ratepayers of three years' standing in the town.[12] The crucial effect of these measures was to separate the freemen from the corporation and create two distinct bodies where only one had existed before. Henceforth the corporation's basic duty would be to the town in general, while the freemen would have a duty only to themselves.

A particularly contentious aspect of the 1835 bill when it was going through parliament had been its proposal that all property held by the old corporations would be handed over to the new corporations. The freemen petitioned parliament that this would 'deprive their Infant Children and Apprentices and their Descendants of their vested rights'. As a result of the wide-scale lobbying from many freemen corporations throughout the country, the bill was amended to the effect that the personal rights and privileges of the country's freemen were to be safeguarded.[13] In Grimsby this had two effects: one was that the freemen retained the right of free education for their children at the corporation's expense. But the other effect was much more important. This was that, although all the corporation land did indeed pass into the ownership of the new reformed corporation, the freemen retained the right to take the benefit from land that they had been using in common and from which they had been taking personal benefits, i.e. the East Marsh, the Little Field and the Haycroft. Thus, even though the corporation owned the land, the freemen set up a committee to administer what they now referred to as 'their' land.

A further divergence of the estate interests of the corporation and the freemen occurred in 1839 in regard to the leasing of the grazing plots in the West Marsh and East End Closes. There was a general shortage of pasture and meadow in the town and, consequently, some freemen were unlawfully allowing their names to be used as 'fronts' by non-freemen who needed pasture land. Accordingly, the reformed corporation asked for permission from the Treasury to open up the bidding to all inhabitants of the town. The freemen objected but the Treasury agreed with the corporation, with the added stipulation that in future lessees need not even be inhabitants of Grimsby. Thus, the freemen henceforth had no rights in the West Marsh and the East End Closes, which the decision of the Treasury had placed firmly in full ownership of the corporation. The first auction under this ruling took place in 1841 when 242 acres of the West Marsh and East End Closes were leased to the general public.[14]

Corporation and Freemen Divided

The cumulative effect of these three acts of parliament and the freemen's subsequent loss of their monopoly of leasing the West Marsh and the East End Closes was to create a sense among the freemen that they had been unjustly treated and deposit a sizeable chip on their shoulders. They felt that they had been misled over the benefits and costs of

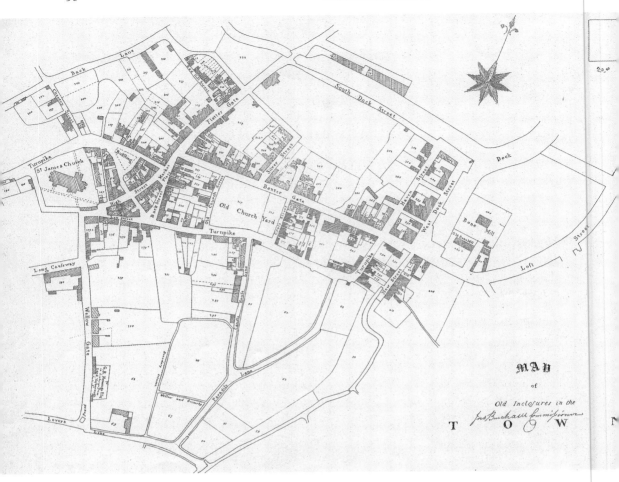

16   *The extent of building in the old town in the 1830s.*

enclosure and that the two reform acts had deprived them of most of their ancient rights and privileges. The most important and far-reaching effects were caused by the municipal reform act. No longer did the freemen comprise the corporation and have the power, influence and benefits that the position had given them. In future, the corporation and the freemen were two quite separate bodies. But despite this, the freemen succeeded in gaining a strong voice in the new reformed corporation. At the first election for the new borough council's 12 councillors, held in December 1835, the freemen fought a vigorous contest and succeeded in getting at least seven of the 12 seats on the council.[15] The freemen continued to maintain a sizeable representation on the borough council and were not hesitant about working on the council in the interests of their fellow freemen.

Chapter 4

Railway and Conflict

1835-1849

Unlikely as it may seem, the provisions of the 1835 municipal reform act were to create serious complications when the railway reached Grimsby. These will be explained later in this chapter but first we have to consider why and how the railway came to Grimsby.

By Rail to Grimsby

The initial interest of railway promoters was in a railway that would serve as a trading link between a port on the East Coast and the manufacturing districts of Lancashire, Yorkshire and the Midlands. In 1831, the Grimsby municipal corporation agreed to 'render every facility to such an undertaking'. The corporation's support is not surprising because the proposed railway would provide the communication with a manufacturing area that the port lacked.[1]

Progress on the railway had to wait until 1844. In October of that year notification was given of a proposed railway, the Great Grimsby and Sheffield Junction Railway (GG&SJR), which would run from Grimsby to Gainsborough, where it would connect with a line to Sheffield. It was promoted by a group of Sheffield men but its provisional committee was headed by Lord Yarborough (1781-1846). He was the son of Charles Anderson Pelham, the 1st Baron Yarborough, whom we have met previously as one of the supporters of the haven dock project. This new head of the family gained even further prestige when he was elevated in rank to become the 1st Earl of Yarborough in 1837. A public meeting to launch the railway was held at the *Red Lion Hotel* in Caistor on 28 October 1844. Presided over by Yarborough, the meeting was well attended by north Lincolnshire landowners who agreed unanimously to the proposed railway. The route was agreed at a meeting in the Grimsby Town Hall on the following 6 November and the GG&SJR Act received the royal assent on 30 June 1845.[2]

Improved dock facilities were to be an integral part of the railway venture and, under the Grimsby Docks Act of 8 August in the same year, the Grimsby Haven Company was dissolved and vested in a new undertaking, the Grimsby Docks Company. Lord Worsley (1809-62), the eldest son of the 1st Earl of Yarborough, was appointed chairman of both the GG&SJR and the Grimsby Docks Company and four other directors were also on the boards of both companies, including local landowners Richard Thorold and George Heneage. It is, therefore, not surprising that at the first general meeting of the Grimsby Docks Company shareholders on 7 October 1845, it was agreed that it should amalgamate with the GG&SJR. The following day saw a decision to start the dock works at once, superintended by James Meadows Rendel as engineer (annual salary £1,000) and Adam Smith as resident engineer (annual salary £500).[3]

From its inception, the GG&SJR was seen as the eastern section of a railway that would run across the country from the Mersey to the Humber. The railways involved in the venture were the Sheffield, Ashton-under-Lyne and Manchester Railway, the Sheffield and Lincolnshire Junction Railway, the Sheffield and Lincolnshire Extension Railway and the GG&SJR, plus the all-important Grimsby Docks Company. These companies were all formally amalgamated by an act of parliament in 1846 as the Manchester, Sheffield & Lincolnshire Railway Company (MS&LR) which came into being on 1 January 1847.[4] It would run from Manchester through Sheffield and Gainsborough to Grimsby, where it would connect with the large new dock that would be constructed as an integral part of the scheme.

The MS&LR's initial board of directors elected as chairman Lord Worsley (now Lord Yarborough, 2nd Earl of Yarborough, after the death of his father in 1846). The board set up two management committees, the Western and Eastern Section Committees. Yarborough was on both committees and the eastern committee also included George Heneage and Richard Thorold. The election of a Lincolnshire peer as chairman of a company with overwhelmingly Manchester and Sheffield connections is intriguing. His prestigious title, his national and parliamentary connections, his position as the leading landowner in northern Lincolnshire and Grimsby and his detachment from sectional interests in Lancashire and Yorkshire would all have been in his favour. From his own standpoint, he probably had mixed motives for taking up the position. These could include a personal sense of duty to the locality, coupled with a realisation that a successful railway would forward the development of his estates and could also be a good investment; in 1850 he remarked that he was the third-largest shareholder in the MS&LR.[5]

Other promoters were also interested in running a railway into Grimsby and, in 1846, formed the East Lincolnshire Railway Company (ELR) with the intention of constructing a line from Grimsby to Louth and Boston. The GG&SJR, and later the MS&LR, tried to acquire or lease the ELR. However, they were opposed by the Great Northern Railway (GNR), which took a lease of the line in 1847 and linked it, via Peterborough, to London. The link to London was all-important. In its petition to parliament in support of the bill setting up the ELR, the corporation's interest in the commerce of the town led it to state that the railway would halve the time it took to get fish from the Humber to London.[6] Public rail services began in Grimsby on 1 March 1848 when the MS&LR and GNR began to run trains on a joint basis between Louth and New Holland via Grimsby. The MS&LR line between Grimsby and Manchester was opened to the public on 17 July 1849. So the MS&LR and GNR lines into Grimsby were soon providing the port with important connections to northern and midland industrial areas and London.

But what of the serious complications that were mentioned at the beginning of this chapter? To explain this we have to go back a few years. Obviously, land was needed in Grimsby for railway lines. The complications arose because the MS&LR needed 36 acres running through the Haycroft, Little Field and East Marsh. This land was the cause of a bitter conflict. We have seen that the Haycroft and Little Field were added to the corporation estate during the process of parliamentary enclosure. We then saw that the freemen decided in 1829 to use this additional land as common pasture, like the East Marsh land. Subsequently, the terms of the 1835 reform act confirmed the corporation as the owner of the land but granted the right to benefit from it to the freemen, who were

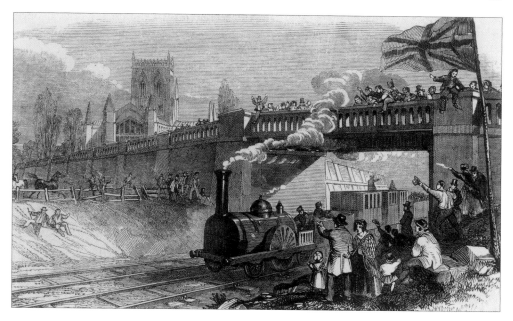

17   *Cheering crowds welcome the beginning of railway services in Grimsby in 1848. Full main line services began the following year and marked the onset of the town's modern growth and success.*

currently using it as common pasture. Thus the corporation and freemen each had an interest in the land that the railway company required. The company would have to pay for the land but the question was, who would receive the money, the corporation or the freemen? And, if both, in what proportion?

Rights and No Surrender

The issue could have been dealt with by the corporation and freemen reaching agreement after rational discussion. This was not to be and the freemen issued a declamatory and confrontational notice[7] on the first day of 1847: 'To the Free Burgesses of the Borough of Great Grimsby and the Widows and Daughters of such Freemen, being entitled by Charter, By Usage, by Bye Law and by the Municipal Reform Act of Parliament to the Freemen's Lands within the said Borough.'

It went on to declare that a committee had been elected for the purpose of meeting with the borough council regarding the price to be paid for the 'Freemen's Lands', and cast a jibe that the corporation 'has not one shilling property either real or personal under their charge but what belongs to the same freemen, not even the Salary of the Mayor or even the lowest officer in the Corporation'.

The notice went on to say that the committee had sent a memorial to the Treasury in London stating their rights and challenged the town council to do the same. The notice also said the committee was prepared to go to law over the matter and 'the Town Council shall not usurp any of your Rights and Privileges, which they [the committee] are determined to support to the utmost extremity'. This declamatory and combative attitude would appear time and time again whenever the freemen felt that their remaining rights and privileges

18   *Grimsby Town Station and a horse and carriage, c.1911.*

were under threat. The corporation's response was muted. It did memorialise the Treasury but confined itself to saying that the freemen claimed the entire compensation for the land required by the MS&LR, but if the corporation received any compensation it would spend it on improving the drainage and sewerage of the town. The Treasury showed a marked lack of interest in the matter and the MS&LR was given access to the land later in the year pending resolution of the issue.[8]

The freemen's committee also issued a call to get freemen elected on to the borough council at the next municipal election in November 1847, when four seats would be up for contest. The freemen had maintained their presence on the council since getting such a strong representation in 1835. By packing the council with more freemen, there was increased likelihood of it agreeing to the freemen's claims. After the initial excitement of the 1835 election, interest had waned among the general body of the electorate and by the mid-1840s there was little competition for council seats. In 1845, only 27 votes were cast for each of four candidates, all of whom were elected and of whom three were freemen. In 1846 only 21 electors bothered to vote for four candidates, all of whom were elected and at least two of whom were freemen. Thus, the large number of freemen on the council explains the muted response of the corporation to the freemen's claims.[9] However, the freemen's new election campaign started in earnest in September 1847 when they issued a notice[10] that indicated clearly that they would treat the election as a fight for their rights:

> To the Freemen of Great Grimsby. The time has now fully arrived when you are called upon to assert your rights ... The question now resolves itself to this EITHER YOU HAVE RIGHTS AND PRIVILEGES OR YOU HAVE NOT; IF YOU HAVE, PLACE THOSE MEN IN THE COUNCIL WHO WILL FEARLESSLY ASSERT THEM.

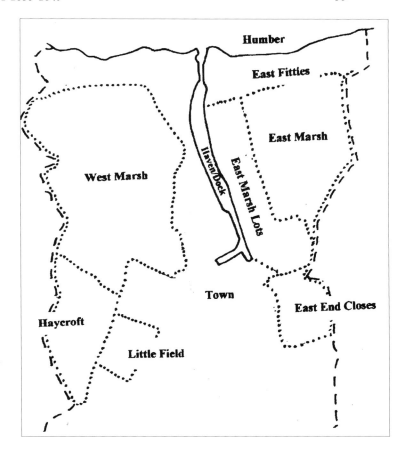

19 *The division of the corporation estate after 1835 into the freemen's estate (consisting of the East Marsh, the Haycroft and the Little Field) and the municipal corporation estate (consisting of the West Marsh, the East End Closes, the East Marsh Lots and the East Fitties).*

The notice then went on to claim the whole of the compensation for the land. There was also clear resentment at what they regarded as the unjust treatment meted out to them in the recent past:

> Years have rolled on and rights have been wrung from you; let not the doings of the year 1847 be handed down to your posterity as the year in which you allowed to pass away that which you can never regain. Be prepared then, Brother Freemen, to attend a meeting to be held next Tuesday evening September 14th.

The tone of confrontation was increased to one of outright battle at the subsequent meeting:

> 'On that evening a band of music was engaged and boards were carried through the town on one of which was inscribed 'Rights and No Surrender'. The freemen afterwards met ... [and] It is expected that there will be some stir on the election of councillors.'[11]

By encouraging confrontation, the freemen certainly created interest in the election. However, a significant effect of their militant style was to emphasise the conflict of interests between themselves and the rest of the townspeople. The electoral turnout was up tenfold on previous elections. This emphasised not only the split in the town between freemen and others but also the importance attached by the townspeople to the issue of compensation for the land, and whether the money should benefit the freemen only or the town generally. From the freemen's point of view they were successful in getting another freeman on to the council. They were now in a very strong position, holding at least eight seats out of the 16 places on the council.[12]

By mid-1848 the payment to be made by the MS&LR had been fixed at £17,000 and was lodged for the time being in a Bank of England account. The freemen's committee took the initiative by issuing a notice in June that maintained their claim to the entire compensation. They then took a major step forward by broadening the issue to include the question of the ownership of land 'from which you [the freemen] have received a benefit from time immemorial'. They stated that they were 'preparing a Scheme which shall not only incorporate such property, but secure an undisturbed possession and absolute control over the same'. The committee finished off the notice by reaffirming their determination to safeguard the rights not only of the freemen but also of their children.[13]

The Freemen's Victory

The overriding impression of the scheme that the freemen then put forward was its overwhelming bias in their favour. Its contents may be divided into four main components. The first component was that there was only token financial recognition of the corporation as the owner of the pastures – it would receive only one-twentieth (five per cent) of the £17,000. Similarly, it would receive one-twentieth of the proceeds of the letting, leasing or sale of the pastures. The remaining nineteen-twentieths (95 per cent) of the £17,000 would be invested and the annual dividends shared equally among the freemen and freemen's widows, as would the nineteen-twentieths of the annual proceeds of letting, leasing or selling the pastures. The second component was that the freemen would be allowed to sell or lease the pastures for building. The third component was that the freemen would be in control of running the pastures by way of general meetings of freemen and a committee of freemen, which would be known as the Pastures Committee. The fourth component was that all the freemen's financial and legal affairs and instructions regarding the pastures would be carried out by the corporation: the mayor would preside at meetings of freemen; the Town Hall would be the venue for their meetings; the town clerk and borough treasurer would act as the freemen's clerk and treasurer and the corporation would obtain the act of parliament necessary for putting the scheme into effect. The stipulations in this fourth component appear to stress that, although the freemen may have been pushed to one side in 1835, they believed that they still had an historical right to be part of the apparatus of local government and were re-establishing their connection.[14]

The Pastures Act, 1849

This scheme was then incorporated into a parliamentary private bill that was approved by the borough council on 12 March 1849 and received the royal assent on 24 May with the short title of the Pastures Act, 1849. The act confirmed that, although the corporation owned the East Marsh, Haycroft and Little Field, that body would effectively merely act as trustees of the land on behalf of the freemen. Under the act the new 'landowner' consisted of those freemen and freemen's widows who were resident in the borough of Grimsby and were entered on a register of resident freemen. This was the Pastures Roll, which was to be revised annually. All those on the roll in any one year were known as the enrolled freemen and widows, and only they could participate in the running of the freemen's pastures and share in the benefits arising from them during that year. The act gave the freemen all the powers of a landowner in deciding how to manage and develop their estate. The corporation was devoid of any powers relating to the pastures and was merely given the duty of carrying out the freemen's instructions.[15]

How Did the Freemen Achieve Victory?

For all practical purposes the original corporation estate had now been divided between the corporation and the freemen. The freemen had become, in effect, the proprietors of an estate of some 170 acres (206 acres less the 36 acres purchased by the MS&LR) and entitled to 95 per cent of all benefits arising from it. In similar cases in the rest of the country there does not appear to be any parallel to the insignificant share to be paid to the corporation, so how did it come about?[16]

A possible answer may be found in the terms of the Clee parliamentary enclosure, which took place during 1842-6. As Lord of the Manor of Clee, the mayor and bailiffs of Grimsby had a manorial interest in the land of that parish and in 1842 the mayor and the town clerk (George Babb) agreed to accept for the corporation the customary manorial grant of one-twentieth of the 'Waste and Commonable Lands' in Clee.[17] This may have provided the basis of Babb's later proposal in the freemen's scheme. However, there is no parallel between the Clee enclosure agreement and the freemen's scheme. The Grimsby corporation was the legal owner of all the land that was being disputed in Grimsby whereas the freemen only had an interest in the land. Consequently, it could be argued that the corporation should have got the lion's share of any settlement and the freemen the smaller share.

More noteworthy than legal technicalities, though, is the corporation's meek acceptance of the freemen's scheme. Why did it give in so quickly and not stand up for the rights of the majority of the ratepayers? We have seen how the freemen mounted a vociferous and vigorous campaign, laying particular emphasis on threats to their inherited rights and privileges. In 1903, the *Grimsby News* contained a lurid account of some of the tactics employed by the freemen to get the Pastures Act agreed:

> It was unopposed, and why? Because no one dare oppose it then [1849]. All knew perfectly well [that] to do so was to be ruined in trade and prospects, if not something more unpleasant; at least you would be likely to be bullied, screamed at, or, a taste of a cow-hide. A ratepayer now living had to protect himself by a heap of stones from being thrown into the dock by a gang of freemen, because he dared to speak his mind fairly and candidly.[18]

Although this and other stories may have become exaggerated in the re-telling, there is no doubt that the freemen were belligerent in their campaign. Also working in their favour was the corporation's town clerk, George Babb the younger. He was a freeman who had been brought up as an involved member of the freemen body. He had been an alderman of the old corporation until becoming town clerk in 1824 on the death of his father. He remained town clerk until his death in 1861. He practised as a solicitor and was also legal advisor to the freemen, subsequently holding the post of clerk to the freemen from 1849 until his death. His role was pivotal in their eventual success.

In July 1848, Babb attended a meeting of freemen and 'recommended such steps to be taken for the skilful management of their funds and Commonable lands as met with the entire concurrence of the Freemen'.[19] In doing this he was more loyal to the freemen than to the corporation. The corporation maintained that it had municipal uses in mind for the MS&LR purchase money but was confounded by its own town clerk, Babb, and others,

20   *On 28 June 1849 the freemen marked the passing of the Pastures Act with this 'Grand Tea Festival' – tickets were one shilling each, tea would be on the table at five o'clock and a band of music would be in attendance.*

who engineered its appropriation for the personal use of the freemen. Thus Babb failed to carry out his municipal duty to the general populace and worked only to the benefit of his fellow freemen. Consequently, when the borough council agreed to the freemen's scheme, they were agreeing to proposals that their own town clerk, himself a freeman, had either drafted or at least helped to formulate. In addition, the colourful and idiosyncratic local historian and freeman Bob Lincoln, writing in 1913, also gave credit to Babb's partner, solicitor William Grange (1821-1913), stating that prior to Babb's death, Grange:

> had been for some years, looking after the destinies of the Freemen, and, without beating about the bush, it is an absolute certainty that to him, for being the guiding light in framing the Act of 1849 and the destinies of the Freemen at this critical period, the present and the future generations too owe him a debt of gratitude which can never be repaid.[20]

The final point in the freemen's favour was the composition of the borough council. The council of August 1848 included at least eight freemen out of a total of 16 members. It met on 11 August to consider the freemen's scheme. At this all-important meeting at least seven freemen were present out of a total attendance of thirteen. Not surprisingly, the meeting approved the scheme. Coincidentally, at the meeting on 12 March 1849, which approved the Pastures Bill, at least seven freemen were present out of a total attendance of thirteen. So at each of these meetings, the freemen were in the majority.[21] There is no doubt that the freemen had a right to share in the increased value of the pastures that was created by the railway and dock development. However, their success in achieving an outcome overwhelmingly in their favour was achieved by a combination of indignation, self-interest, pugnacious determination and influential allies in the right positions. Even the smooth passage of the bill through parliament was aided by gaining the support of the local Member of Parliament, George Heneage. This was achieved by including in the act permission for him to have road access into Grimsby (along Pasture Street) from his Weelsby estate; a benefit that he had been trying to acquire for many years. Despite this parliamentary help, Bob Lincoln, possibly quoting his father, acknowledged that the bill was enacted 'to the astonishment of all'.[22]

The New Landowner

With the implementation of the Pastures Act a new landowner came into being. It was a corporate landowner that had few, if any, exact counterparts in the kingdom. It was composed of many hundreds of freemen who gave the corporate body its own distinctive personality. It was democratic in that each freemen, whatever his social or economic standing, had an equal vote in deciding its policy. And, importantly, its corporate duty was towards the well-being of the freemen only. Finally, and this had nothing to do with the Pastures Act, freemen could stand for election to the borough council and influence council decisions. Accordingly, in view of the effect that this landowner was to have on the building of the town, it is essential to examine it and its members, the freemen, in some detail.

The freemen came from a varied social and economic background, as has been outlined above. At one extreme were sober and staid individuals such as the freemen's clerk and treasurer, William Grange and Thomas Stephenson, both of whom were Methodists and teetotallers. At the other extreme were individuals such as William Colley Parker, later referred to as a reformed drunkard. His exploits included, in 1857, leading a gang of freemen and others in destroying a barricade put up by the railway company in an argument over the payment of tolls to use a wharf. It was reported a couple of months later that 'This notorious character was imprisoned on Tuesday last for the 33rd time.' He was reputed to be 'the pet of the people' and crowds turned out to meet him on his release from prison in 1860.[23] Similar members of the freemen body were highlighted in a newspaper report about the distribution of the dividend at the Town Hall in 1882, which painted a lengthy and uncomplimentary picture of some freeman types. The reporter commented that it was hardly surprising that 'a very select class' deputised someone to fetch their dividend for them.[24] Indeed, there is no doubt that many freemen must have been embarrassed by the behaviour of some of their number. However, it does illustrate the diverse make-up of this landowner that would have such a say in expanding the built-up area of the town.

The Pastures Committee

The overall authority in the freemen's affairs was the full body of freemen assembled either at their annual meeting in June or at special meetings that were called to resolve important or contentious issues. At the annual meeting the freemen elected the committee of 14 freemen that was known as the Pastures Committee. The committee's function was to supervise and manage the affairs of the freemen but always 'subject to such regulations and restrictions as the enrolled freemen from time to time determine'.[25] Thus, the whole body of the freemen kept ultimate control as they had done when they comprised the Full Court of the old borough council.

The freemen held their first annual meeting under the Pastures Act in 1849 and elected the first Pastures Committee. A county newspaper expected that the committee would have a difficult time pleasing the freemen and that it could 'expect plenty of work and no pay'.[26] Of the 14 members, eight had been on the freemen's committee that led the belligerent and successful campaign against the corporation over the pastures. They could thus be expected to have an uncompromising attitude on meeting the needs of the freemen. The members were from middle-ranking occupations and included a draper, druggist, coal merchant, baker, blacksmith, merchant, block maker, wheelwright, butcher, schoolmaster, two ironmongers and two builders. Two members of the committee were also on the borough council, thereby providing a direct voice for the committee in council deliberations.[27]

The chairman of the Pastures Committee was elected annually. His character and personality could affect how the estate was administered. Two men in particular epitomised the character of those holding office and between them they dominated the post of chairman during the later 19th century. For most of the period 1864-99 they led the Pastures Committee, being in office between them for 31 of the 35 years. John Barker (1823-96) was chairman in 1871-85. He had been employed with William Grange in the solicitor's office of George Babb. He left to work for the Hull Banking Company and when he retired in 1891, as manager of the Grimsby branch, had been in their employment for up to 40 years. He was also chairman of the Grimsby Gas Company. He was a magistrate, a strict Primitive Methodist and a Liberal.[28] For the last five years of his life he was a borough councillor. When he was elected to the borough council the *Grimsby Observer*, a Conservative paper, remarked on his 'crotchety ideas' and commented that:

The general opinion seems to be that he will not be long in displaying them, for having held a somewhat despotic position in two or three semi-public capacities, the natural bent of his mind ... may lead to unusual conflict of opinion and unpleasant personal animosities ... [we] hope he will not attempt inside to thwart the corporation as he has done outside.[29]

The other long-serving chairman was John Neville Chapman (1824-99) who held the position in 1864-7 and 1885-99. He had been educated with William Grange at the freemen's school in Grimsby. He became manager of the Grimsby Waterworks Company from its formation in 1864 until he retired in 1884. He was a Wesleyan Methodist. On his death a local newspaper remarked: 'We should think everybody is acquainted with the aggressive Freeman as typified in Mr Chapman. He thoroughly believed in the "Divine right" of the Pastures Committee.'[30]

The freemen's clerk was a pivotal figure in that he was their legal advisor and executive officer as well as their link with the corporation. The first clerk, George Babb the younger, held the post for 11 years. He must occupy an important place in the freemen's pantheon of heroes in that he was instrumental in getting the favourable terms of the Pastures Act drawn up and enacted. However, his successor was more significant in the long-term development of the freemen's estate. This was his business partner William Grange, who was town clerk and clerk to the freemen for the 52-year period 1861-1913, dying in office at the age of 91 – no sign of ageism in Victorian and Edwardian Grimsby. Accordingly, he had the dubious distinction of being the oldest town clerk in the country and for more than half a century was the legal advisor and chief executive officer for both the corporation and the freemen during one of the most important periods of Grimsby's urban development.

The Freemen and the Annual Dividend

Under the Pastures Act, the monies arising from the pastures would be shared equally among the enrolled freemen and freemen's widows in the form of an annual dividend, although it was actually distributed in two parts in June and November. This dividend had a significant influence on the development of the freemen's estate because the greater the profit from the land, the higher would be the sum available for sharing out. A recurring theme during the century was the freemen's preoccupation with the annual dividend. This is not surprising because to a working man the amounts were significant and grew as the freemen's estate was turned over to housing. Accordingly, an annual increase came to be expected and a decrease was looked upon as extremely unwelcome. In the year 1857 there were 449 freemen, their estate produced £557, and they each got a dividend of £1 4s. 0d. By 1880 their numbers had increased to 708, their income had risen more than sixfold to £3,610 and the dividend had increased nearly fourfold to £4 11s. 0d. This was to prove the high point of the dividend for many years to come. By 1910 their numbers had increased to 1,248 and because their estate income had not risen in proportion the dividend had fallen to £2 19s. 0d.[31]

The diverse nature of the freemen influenced their preoccupation with the dividend. We have seen that a large number were in unskilled occupations and there is no doubt that a sizeable number of freemen and freemen's widows welcomed the dividend as help in straitened circumstances. A press report during a very cold January in 1861 stated that an extraordinary dividend would be paid as soon as possible 'so that those in need may feel the benefit of this excellent fund'. At a time when local bricklayers and dock labourers could expect to earn in the region of four shillings a day, the dividend represented a helpful sum of money.[32]

However, some freemen criticised their fellows' undue concern with the dividend, with such comments as: 'They seem to be perfectly satisfied so long as they receive their dividend and that there is some little increase.'[33] A striking instance of this attitude occurred in the year 1859-60 when the Pastures Committee reduced the dividend considerably because they had used £693 from the freemen's income to pay the cost of laying out the East Marsh for building. As a result the disgruntled freemen removed most of them from office at the next annual election. During the following year the new Pastures Committee sold sufficient securities to be able to retrieve the £693 and pay an extra dividend to make up for the shortfall in the previous year.[34] The question of the dividend became central to the actions of the Pastures Committee, which was concerned to keep the freemen happy by maintaining a high income and low expenditure.

Chapter 5

Railway Port

1849-1880s

Although the shenanigans over land and money may have occupied the time and energy of the corporation and freemen, the MS&LR was more interested in railway and dock construction and the prospects for a revitalised Grimsby, 'which it is hardly possible at present adequately to appreciate; but which must in a few years become the scene of extensive commerce, and in times, whether of peace or war, of great national importance'.[1]

The investment and enterprise of the railway company would certainly be needed if we trust the comments of a smart alick journalist who described the town in 1849 as 'one of those places that few of our readers have heard of ... but which I can best describe as a place that a London contractor would cart away in three weeks'.[2]

Royal Dock

The railway line to Manchester was opened in 1849 but it would be three more years before the dock was completed. It was designed by one of the century's premier civil engineers, James Meadows Rendel (1799-1856). His plan for Grimsby was 'a magnificent piece of compact engineering which went ahead almost without a hitch'. The old haven dock was ignored because of its silting problems and the new dock was built on new land that was reclaimed from the Humber mudflats. Work began in the spring of 1846 with the construction of a huge coffer dam, taking in 138 acres, which stretched three-quarters of a mile out into the Humber and was regarded as 'one of the wonders of the age'.[3] The dam and the integral embankment and wharf were finished by the end of 1848 and the dock's foundation stone was to be laid the following year at the base of one of the lock pits. Prince Albert, the Prince Consort, had agreed to perform the ceremony. The impending royal visit caused a stir. The mayor requested that the day of the visit be a public holiday and that all shops be closed. A celebration public ball was organised. A subscription was set up so that foodstuffs might be distributed to the poor. Possibly the spirit of the occasion is best summed up in the following extract from a poem written and published at the time by one W. Botterill to mark the visit:

> Honour'd Prince, with joy we greet thee!
> Tens of thousands of our race
> Come in one vast group to meet thee –
> To behold thy royal face.

Welcome! Welcome!
Welcome to this rising place!

Beauteous banners now are flying,
Sweet musicians march along;
Bells are ringing – people crying
With one simultaneous tongue,
ROYAL STRANGER!
Welcome to our festive throng!

Costly fireworks, rich and splendid,
Will display their vivid light –
Shine in various colours blended –
Radiate the gloom of night
Welcome! Welcome!
Welcome to this glorious sight!

This went on for another eight verses, welcoming the Prince and saying how the port would thrive and prosper henceforth.[4]

We do not know if the Prince saw the poem (or what he thought of it) but, after an overnight stay at Lord Yarborough's Brocklesby Hall, his special train passed under a

21　*Construction of the Royal Dock, c.1850; by J.W. Carmichael. (From a painting at the Institution of Civil Engineers.)*

triumphal arch as it arrived at Grimsby station on 18 April 1849. Following a welcome by local dignitaries the train passed under two more triumphal arches on its way to the dock entrance. Then the engine was unhitched and a hundred navvies in 'short white smocks and nightcaps' pulled the train to the site of the ceremony.[5] It was reported that:

> Throughout the morning trains and boats, crammed to capacity, had been decanting human cargoes at Grimsby, and the amphitheatre was crowded by the time the Prince was due to arrive. The spectators had been drenched by a ten-minute cloudburst, but the downpour had ceased before the Prince and his entourage descended to the scene of action, accompanied by a roar of cheering and the booming of a royal salute ... After the stone had been laid the Sheerness squadron of the Royal Navy anchored in the roadstead fired several salvoes.[6]

The Prince and Lord Yarborough and 1,000 guests adjourned for lunch at a pavilion erected nearby. In his speech the Prince said:

> We have been laying the foundation stone of a dock, not only as a place of safety, refuge, and refitment for our mercantile marine, and calculated to receive the largest steamers of Her Majesty's navy, but it may, and I trust it will, be the foundation of a great commercial port.[7]

The Prince then made his way back to London in his special train – and sent £50 for the navvies in their white smocks and nightcaps. By then they would no doubt have discarded this fetching attire and got on with completing the dock and its two locks, the larger of which could accommodate the biggest warships of the day. The lock gates and dockside cranes were operated by hydraulic pressure. In his work elsewhere, Rendel had already 'acquired that mastery of hydraulic engineering on which his fame chiefly rests'. For his work at Grimsby, he received a grand medal of honour at the Paris exhibition of 1855. Sir William Armstrong of Newcastle perfected the technique and the machinery used at Grimsby; Grimsby was the first port to have a full hydraulic system operating. This and the dock's 'superb integration with a railway' have led to it being called the first truly modern dock in Britain. Hydraulic pressure was supplied from a tank holding 33,000 gallons of water and fixed 200 feet above ground in the dock's distinctive tower. The design of the tower, by architect J.W. Wild, is based on the tower of the Palazzo Pubblico in Siena, Italy. It was completed on 27 March 1852 and is 309 feet high to the top of its lantern. However, even while it was under construction Armstrong was developing an alternative hydraulic system using accumulators. A much lower hydraulic accumulator tower on the opposite side of the lock became operational in 1892. The dock was 20 acres in extent plus a timber pond of five acres. Outside the dock gates was a tidal basin of 13 acres bounded by two timber piers. All this was costing a lot of money; the total outlay would eventually be about £1,050,000.[8] Not surprisingly, the MS&LR directors were concerned to keep the confidence of the shareholders and reported to them in 1850 that:

> Nothing has occurred to shake the confidence they have always felt in the ultimate success of this great national undertaking. From their superior convenience, ready access, and contiguity to the sea, they cannot fail to acquire a considerable portion of the present trade of the Humber, and a large share of its annually increasing commerce, for they will be the only Docks on the eastern coast capable of admitting the large class of steam vessels now employed in the trade of northern Europe.[9]

22   *River trip from Hull on Good Friday 1852 to view Grimsby's new dock.*

The opening of the dock took place in 1852. On 18 March, to mark the dock's completion, the larger of the two lock pits was the unlikely venue for another sumptuous banquet. Three hundred or more guests were seated in a large marquee. Guests included the chairman of the MS&LR, Lord Yarborough, and local civic leaders. The banquet lasted four and a half hours. It concluded after the 15th toast, by which time 'not a few of the guests must have experienced some difficulty in negotiating the long improvised staircases which rose up from the lock pit to the dockside'. Water was let into the dock on 22 March and it was opened for use on 27 May. The mayor once again requested local businesses to make the day a general holiday and the celebrations included a procession from the Town Hall to the dock.[10]

The dock became 'royal' more than two years after its opening. Queen Victoria, Prince Albert and family members called at Hull and Grimsby on their way to London from Scotland. On 14 October

23   *A busy Riverhead c. 1890s. Despite the construction of new docks, the Riverhead continued to be used by river and coastal traffic.*

1854 they left Hull's Corporation Pier on the royal yacht Fairy and arrived at Grimsby's new dock soon after 12.30 p.m. They were greeted by Lord Yarborough and the Grimsby mayor and corporation and inspected the dock works. The Queen agreed to a request that the dock should be named 'Royal Dock' in honour of her visit. The two eldest royal children seized the opportunity to ascend by the hydraulic lift to the top of the dock tower, accompanied by Prince Albert and James Rendel, after which the royal party proceeded to Grimsby railway station for the journey to London by the GNR royal train. During the decade 1853-63, the number of vessels calling at Grimsby to and from foreign ports grew from 530 to 1,367 and their total tonnage grew from 134,334 to 317,593. The tonnage of cargo was also increasing rapidly; in 1865, 181,352 tons of timber were imported and, in 1864, 155,205 tons of coal were exported.[11]

24 Sir Edward Watkin, chairman of the MS&LR 1864-94. He was credited with the rise of the port in the 19th century and rewarded with the honorary freedom of the borough in 1891.

Sir Edward Watkin

It was after the railway and dock were in operation that a man appeared on the scene who was to have a dominant role in the MS&LR and, consequently, in the growth of Grimsby. This was Edward William Watkin (1819-1901) who was the eldest son of a prominent Manchester cotton merchant. He left the family business in 1845 to enter the railway industry and was appointed the MS&LR's general manager on 1 January 1854. He held the post until late 1861 when he resigned over a disagreement about policy. He returned in 1863 on being elected to the board of directors and was then elected chairman of the company in 1864. He held this position until 1894 when he resigned because of ill health, but remained on the board. He thus had a central role in the development of the MS&LR and Grimsby over five decades of their most formative period.[12]

He soon made his mark in 1854 and, 'With the advent of Watkin it quickly became evident that a progressive and enlightened policy was to be pursued with both the business community and the [railway] staff.'[13] Such was his energy and reputation that he became the 'Railway King' of the later 19th century and while running the MS&LR was also the chairman of several other railway companies. In addition, he carried out important work in Canada for the British government and was knighted in 1868. During the 1880s he was in the forefront of schemes to construct a Channel Tunnel as part of his vision of running through trains from Manchester to the Continent and beyond. His ambition that the MS&LR should have its own main line to London was achieved in 1899, the company having changed its name to the Great Central Railway (GCR) in 1898 to mark its enlarged sphere of operation.

Fishing and Fish Docks

The idea of reviving the local fishing trade was being discussed before the railway was built. Evidence was given to the Tidal Harbours Commission in 1845 that 80 or 90 fishing boats could be seen in the Humber at any one time but most of the fish was taken to Hull, which had had a railway since 1840:

> If there was a railroad from Grimsby, fish might, on some occasions, be in London by it before they could get to Hull: there is twelve hours difference, at certain times, between landing the fish at Grimsby and Hull. There is no other port I am acquainted with so convenient as Grimsby's for fishermen landing fish; but fishing smacks don't come to Grimsby, but go to Hull, to enable them to get their fish to the market sooner ... More fishing vessels have gone to Hull since the railway [there] was opened.[14]

After the Royal Dock was completed, the MS&LR continued spending large sums on improving port facilities and encouraging the fishing industry, in conjunction with the GNR and the Midland Railway. The MS&LR's historian, George Dow, has written: 'Perhaps the greatest achievement of the MS&LR at Grimsby was to lay the foundations of an industry which eventually made the name of the town synonymous with fish.'[15] In 1852, 500 tons of fish were sent by rail from Grimsby and in the same year a local directory commented on:

> The great facilities offered by the Great Northern Railway for the conveyance of fish to the London market, combined with the very favourable position of this port for ... the Norway Lobster trade, and the Dogger Bank Cod Fishery ... We have little doubt of this becoming, in the course of a short time, the most important fishing port in England. The Manchester, Sheffield and Lincolnshire Railway Company are forming a Fishing Dock ... where fish can be loaded at once on the railway trucks.[16]

Low dock dues were quoted to attract fishermen from other ports and the construction of a six-acre fish dock was completed in 1856. The rise of the industry was rapid: in 1863 the quantity of fish carried from the port by rail had risen to 10,360 tons and 'Grimsby was preparing to become the greatest fishing port in the world.'[17] The number of fishing vessels belonging to Grimsby in March 1871

25   *Fishing smacks such as the* City of Rome *(pictured here) were the mainstay of the Grimsby fishing industry before the advent of steam trawlers.*

26   *Grimsby cod fishermen, late 19th century.*

(exclusive of the many vessels belonging to other ports but working out of Grimsby) was 303, employing 1,422 men and boys. By March 1880 this had increased to 567 local boats employing 3,070 men and boys.[18] The latter included indentured fishing apprentices. The vast majority were sent to the port from orphanages, workhouses and reformatories throughout the country to meet the rapidly growing industry's shortage of crew members. In his comprehensive, disturbing and critical book on the subject, local fishing historian David Boswell reckoned that more than 9,000 boys were apprenticed to work on Grimsby fishing boats during the period 1868-1900. Some became successful in the industry but others suffered privation, cruelty or death, and many absconded.[19]

Rapidly increasing trade caused the fish dock to be extended. Even so, it soon became inadequate and a second fish dock was opened in 1877, which also had to be extended. Early local experience of using steam-driven vessels in the industry led to the formation in 1881 of the Great Grimsby Steam Trawling Company, which immediately contracted for the supply of two specially designed steam trawlers, the Zodiac and the Aries, constructed at Hull and Grimsby for £3,500 and £3,350 respectively. By 1884 the company had six steam trawlers, and the transformation of the port's fishing fleet from sail to steam had begun. Local boat building had a resurgence, with yards being sited near the entrance to the haven dock. The original dock offices near the lock pits were replaced in 1885 by the present imposing dock offices.[20]

Commercial Docks and Shipping

Such was the increase in commercial traffic that by 1865 Grimsby had become the fifth port in the kingdom, with the value of its export traffic alone exceeding £6.5 million annually. Not surprisingly, the MS&LR needed more dock accommodation and in 1873 paid the corporation £31,500 for 105 acres of the West Marsh for dock extension work. Schemes were then put in hand to improve the haven dock and link it with the Royal Dock. The haven dock was improved and enlarged with the construction of the 26-acre West Arm north of the present Adam Smith Street. The link with the Royal Dock was provided by the construction of the Union Dock, which was opened by the Prince and Princess [Alexandra] of Wales in 1879. They also unveiled a statue of the Prince Consort, which had been paid for by Watkin and his wife. As a result of the royal visit the improved haven dock and its West Arm extension were renamed the Alexandra Dock; the construction work was completed in 1880. In deciding on this project, the MS&LR directors had chosen to disregard a report of their consulting engineer, Charles Liddell. He favoured an entirely new dock being built upstream at Killingholme, rather than at Grimsby. The entrance to a dock at Killingholme would be much nearer to deep water and he estimated the costs of the comparable schemes as £416,000 at Killingholme and £663,000 at Grimsby. Liddell's recommendations would be justified in the following century with the construction of the Immingham Dock.[21]

27 *Sailing ships at Grimsby in the 1870s.*

The MS&LR provided onward transit to continental Europe on both its own boats and those of shipping companies. By 1868 the railway company had its own fleet of 10 vessels sailing to Hamburg, Rotterdam, Antwerp and other northern ports. The fleet was later expanded to 15 vessels and sailings increased to take in more ports in northern Europe and the Baltic. Meanwhile, in 1856, the MS&LR had formed the Anglo-French Steamship Company in association with the South Yorkshire Railway and French coal importers. Under the chairmanship of Lord Yarborough it was created with the aim of exporting South Yorkshire steam coal to French ports.[22]

Grimsby also became one of the links in the journey made by European emigrants, heading mainly for America. The MS&LR ships and others carried migrants from Hamburg and other continental ports to Grimsby. At Grimsby they would mostly entrain for Liverpool and there embark for America. In April 1854 it was reported that over 1,000 emigrants a month were landing from the Hamburg and Rotterdam packets. On one day alone in April 1857, 560 Mormon men, women and children arrived en route for Liverpool and thence to Salt Lake City.[23] In 1871 a local directory commented that:

On the west of the Royal Dock is the old Station for passengers to the Continent, opened by Her Majesty Queen Victoria in 1854. The station is now used for emigrants in transit from the Continent. There is sleeping room for 250 to 300 persons, and private rooms for first-class passengers, in addition to a residence for the interpreter, Mr Isaac Freeman.[24]

The station became known as the Emigrants' Home but most spent just one night there en route to America or towns in this country. The heavy traffic continued into the early years of the next century.

Watkin's Town

As the port and its services were improved and trade increased there were acknowledgements of the part played by Sir Edward Watkin. In 1875 when the corporation was naming new streets on the West Marsh a local newspaper commented on the happy choice of the names of people who had served the town. It remarked in particular that, 'A sense of appreciation has led them to honour ... the Chairman of our Railway and Dock Company' – and so Watkin Street was named.[25] In 1880 Watkin patted himself on the back when he was asked whether he knew about the development of Grimsby. He replied, 'I made it.' This was a sweeping statement but a later comment on him was: 'The town of Grimsby is a standing monument to his judgement and foresight.'[26] In 1881 his efforts in building up the fishing trade were commented on:

He had earned the thanks of Midland and Northern, as well as London ichthyophagi [fish-eaters], by giving them fresh fish in the morning for breakfast. It is not very long since Leeds, Bradford, Huddersfield, York, Derby, Sheffield, and even Manchester and Liverpool, were comparatively fishless places, depending on local supply and London for what little they had ... [but now] the Midlands are at least as well supplied with fish as London. All this is due to Grimsby Docks and the Manchester, Sheffield and Lincoln [sic] Railroad, which was in a poor way when Sir Edward Watkin – first as manager, and then as chairman – took it firmly in hand, and raised the population of Grimsby from eight thousand to forty thousand [sic]. Grimsby now disposes of fish to the extent of fifty-eight thousand tons per annum, a trade actually created by the judgement and foresight of one man.[27]

In 1891, when Grimsby was celebrating the achievement of county borough status, the corporation granted the honorary freedom of the borough to several people to whom it felt gratitude for the advancement of the town. One of these was Sir Edward Watkin and in his case the timing of the occasion was fortuitous because three years later ill health obliged him to retire as chairman of the railway company. Further plaudits followed, on his death in 1901:

> The extraordinary rise of the Port of Grimsby during the last half of the 19th century ... is inseparably connected with the late Sir Edward Watkin ... it was to the personal effort of [him] ... that the increased facilities, the extended dock accommodation and the building up of our fishing and shipping trades were due.[28]

Railway and Town

Having outlined railway and dock development in Grimsby, we can now begin to see how it influenced the built-up nature of 'Watkin's Town'. Firstly, the MS&LR land requirements led to the conversion of the freemen into land developers, whom we will see had a major effect on the urban landscape. Secondly, both the MS&LR and the GNR/ELR cut up the town with their lines creating the need for level crossings and underpasses and causing communication difficulties that still have an effect on traffic routes; at the time of writing the course of the ELR line is used for the Peaks Parkway. Thirdly, the locations of the Alexandra Dock extension and the Royal Dock also affected the town. The former helped to consolidate the uncomfortable mix of residential and industrial development that evolved on the West Marsh, which will be described in chapter ten. The location of the Royal Dock and the fish docks had more acute effects. The decision to create a new dockland by enclosing a large area of mudflats increased the town's acreage and altered its topography. Certainly in modern times it has also denied the townspeople convenient recreational access to the Humber waterfront. But more crucially, its location dictated where the extensive building of working-class housing took place, which will be described in the next chapter when looking at the building on the East Marsh.

Public Health

Although the railway company had this crucial effect on the town, and would continue to affect its development, other forces also produced their own results. One of these was the long-standing tradition of local landed magnates having 'influence' in the town. This was epitomised in a controversy over public health that occurred in mid-century and raises the question of who was actually running the town, the elected borough council or the major landowners. The point at issue was whether the town council should gain extra public health powers by becoming a Local Board of Health (and consequently be supervised by the London-based General Board of Health) or whether it should get similar powers under its own Improvement Act, and remain its own master.

The MS&LR's construction work in Grimsby had led to a rapid increase in population, which itself led to concerns over public health. For example, the town's burial place, St James' churchyard, was noisome and full to overflowing. Consequently, in August 1849, residents petitioned the General Board of Health, asking it to give the town council the added function of being a Local Board of Health. It would then have new powers to create a new cemetery, appoint medical officers, cleanse, pave and sewer the town and provide a water supply. It would also operate under the authority and watchful eye of the General Board of Health.[29]

However, the town clerk, George Babb the younger, thought otherwise. On 24 October 1849 he wrote to the General Board and also issued a public notice to the effect that, instead of becoming a Local Board of Health, the corporation would be applying for a local Improvement Act. Under this act it could, in effect, carry out the functions of a Local Board of Health. It would also have specific powers to enlarge and improve the market place, arrange for the supply of gas and form a new burial ground, which would be partly on the freemen's Little Field. The freemen quickly objected, arguing that a burial ground would decrease the value of their other nearby land and in any case an act of parliament would be unnecessary and expensive to obtain. On 9 November, the town council also objected to Babb's proposed Improvement Act.[30] However, the agents of the two major local landowners, Lord Yarborough and George Heneage, who argued in favour of Babb's proposals, attended a later meeting of the council, on 24 November. Accordingly, the council executed a complete about-face and resolved to join the landowners in supporting Babb's proposed Improvement Act. A public meeting of ratepayers two days later thought differently and supported the creation of a Local Board of Health while opposing the unnecessary expense of an Improvement Act.[31]

This was followed on 14 December by an inquiry into the sanitary condition of the town by a General Board of Health inspector William Ranger. In his report he stressed the need for a new cemetery, the necessity for improved sanitation and the regulation of building and street layout. He noted nine pumps available for public use at the time of his visit and emphasised the need for a supply of water to every house. He also thought that a new market place could be achieved cheaply and effectively without the need for an Improvement Act.[32] Accordingly, against its own inclination, the borough council was created a Local Board of Health on 14 April 1851, and henceforth obliged to carry additional responsibilities.

The council was now wearing two hats. Reluctantly donning its Local Board of Health hat, it appointed the MS&LR docks engineer James Rendel as its consulting engineer but showed no other signs of activity. On 20 October 1852, wearing its borough council hat, it resolved to apply for an Improvement Act. It stated that this was at the behest of the 'proprietors of estates' who wanted an act without delay.[33] The act would include the powers that had already figured in Babb's proposed act. It would also take on board Ranger's comments, make improved police regulations and include authority to create a cemetery, either on the corporation's East End Closes or on Heneage's land off Bargate. Opposition arose again in the town, plus criticism that the proposed site for the cemetery on the corporation land was unsuitable, the idea of using Heneage's land having been dropped.[34]

Despite public opposition, the Improvement Act became law in 1853.[35] There is little doubt that Lord Yarborough and George Heneage were the main driving force in pushing for the act.[36] There is no clear answer to the question as to why this was so. Was it on ideological grounds? At that time there was strong general opposition to any 'interference' by central government in local affairs. In the particular case of Grimsby, Yarborough and Heneage could have viewed the authority wielded by the General Board of Health as weakening their long-standing influence over the corporation. Alternatively, did these two magnates have an altruistic or paternalistic wish to ensure the corporation had the wider-ranging powers for improving the town that the act would provide? Finally, was it for their financial benefit? In order to create the market

28   *The Town Hall, built in 1780, pictured here c.1820. It was located in what became the Old Market Place and is viewed here with Bethlehem Street to the right and the old High Street to the left. It was demolished in 1868 after being replaced by the present Town Hall in 1863.*

place, the corporation had to purchase and demolish 37 properties, 12 of which were owned by Lord Yarborough, for which he was paid £4,570 in 1855.[37] But of much more benefit to Yarborough in particular, and also to Heneage and other interested parties, was the stipulation in the act relating to land used for agriculture, docks and railways, in all of which Yarborough and Heneage had interests. The stipulation was that such land would pay a reduced rate of only one-quarter of the standard municipal rate. Therefore, those with such interests would be paying proportionately less for improvements than other ratepayers.

So after all the fuss, what improvements were actually carried out in the town? The cemetery opened in 1855 on poorly drained corporation land and had persistent problems with drainage, including reports of coffins floating in waterlogged graves. Two years after opening it had become a meeting place for prostitutes and their clients. It is now the recreation ground at the end of Doughty Road. The market place was created, became known as the Old Market Place and was graced with a Corn Exchange, built in 1857. In 1856, authority was received to borrow £16,000 to finance a waterworks and a town drainage scheme but no action followed. A private company provided a waterworks and water supply in 1864 but in 1871 only 1,300 out of over 4,000 houses had a piped water supply. The drainage scheme was replaced by piecemeal work in 1862 costing £974.[38]

The corporation's intrinsic reluctance to act on public health matters was compounded during 1858-60 when the council was dominated by members of a rate-saving Ratepayers Protection Committee. Historian John Newbery, in his detailed work on public health in Grimsby, has summed up the controversy as between the 'clean party' in favour of sanitary reform and led by the landed proprietors and the 'dirty party' obsessed with questions of cost and led by 'petit bourgeois leaders'.[39]

Town Facilities

As the town grew, so did its facilities. The town had had a gas supply since 1836 the first gasworks being set up by Richard Holme of Hull on land near the site of the present Corporation Bridge. A gas company was later established and the plant was moved to the area of Holme Street. The town streets had 103 gas lamps in 1852. By 1877, the gasworks had moved to Sheepfold Street. Other developments in the town included the formation of a four-man police force in 1846. New buildings included the Baptist Chapel in Upper Burgess Street (1838), the Wesleyan Methodist George Street Chapel (1847), the Oddfellows' Hall (1854), the Mechanics' Institute (1856), the Primitive Methodist Victoria Street Chapel (1859) and the establishment of a Savings Bank in 1857 (open twice a week in the Corn Exchange).

As a partial counterbalance to the derogatory comments quoted at the beginning of this chapter, a local directory noted in 1852 that:

29 *The buildings in the centre of the picture were demolished in the mid-19th century to make way for the Old Market Place. The small cupola of the old Town Hall may be seen in the distance. Bethlehem Street is to the left, the old High Street is to the right, from which Butchery Lane leads off to the Bull Ring.*

Within the last few years a succession of events have occurred to make the name of Great Grimsby less absurd ... Very extensive alterations have taken place within a few years, in metamorphosing dwelling houses into shops. Also building new shops with handsome plate-glass windows, indeed, it is supposed that plate-glass windows are more numerous here for the size of the place, than almost any other town in England. There still remains great room for improvement.[40]

Four years later, even more improvements could be reported:

Many of the old and low buildings have given place to spacious houses and shops. Since the opening of the New Docks, several new streets have been opened, and the town is now rapidly improving in size and appearance. During the last five years, several handsome terraces of neat houses have been erected.[41]

Chapter 6

Building the East Marsh
1840s-1870s

The dramatic effect of the MS&LR investment in Grimsby was commented on in 1847: 'This place now presents a most animated appearance. The vast number of men employed at the Railway and Dock works, together with the great influx of strangers and new residents, has caused such a change in the aspect of trade as Grimsby has never witnessed.'[1]

The MS&LR did not see as its concern the provision of housing for this 'great influx of strangers and new residents'. Fortunately, others were more than happy to turn agricultural land over to housing. So began the building of modern Grimsby.

Completing the New Town: East Marsh Lots and East Fitty Lots

It was purely by chance that many building plots were still vacant on the East Marsh Lots and East Fitty Lots – the New Town that had been set out for building by the old corporation in 1800. They were in an ideal location to provide mass working-class housing, being adjacent to railway line workings and handy for both the new dock site and the old haven dock. Accordingly, a building boom ensued on the lots, which were held by many individuals. There is no evidence of local building control so each owner was able to have houses built at a rapid pace to meet the demand for accommodation.

Some of the buildings on the front lots (on Victoria Street North) were commercial premises or were occupied by middle-class families. Householders included Baptist minister William Marjerum who had been born in Great Yarmouth. Another was baker and grocer James Watmough who had several employees. He had been born in Caistor, and his household included his wife (born in Brigg), five children aged two, four, five, seven and ten (all born in Grimsby), four servants (born in Louth, Caistor, Beesby and Deeping) and a journeyman baker born in Louth. Unmarried schoolmistress Mary Coates, born in Sleaford, headed a household consisting of her mother and father, a nephew, two teachers, four pupil boarders and a house servant; no one in the household had been born locally.[2]

In contrast, many of the back lots were quickly turned over to closely packed working-class housing and soon acquired a reputation for containing some of the worst slums in Grimsby. Although not mentioning the East Marsh Lots by name it was reported in 1850 that many owners of small plots of land had 'knocked up a lot of small tenements not fit for dogs to live in'. William Ranger inspected the area during the course of his inquiry for the General Board of Health in 1850. He was particularly critical of the courts and

30   *Victoria Street North in the early 1900s. The buildings are on the East Marsh Front Lots, originally set out for building in 1800. The entrance to the Central Market is just beyond the shop with the full white awning left of centre in the picture.*

back-to-back houses, most of which were on the East Marsh Lots and East Fitty Lots and crammed into the original lots of 360 square yards that had been set out by the old corporation. He thought it essential that regulations 'should be put in force to prevent in future the erection of any dwelling-houses on the defective and faulty principles that have hitherto been followed'.[3]

Examples that he gave included Ellis's Buildings, off Lower Burgess Street, which was entered by a covered passage and contained 12 two-storeyed houses with a ten-foot width between opposing houses. The houses had no back outlet and had been built recently. Sixty people lived in the court. A block of 14 back-to-back houses on another 360-square-yard lot was described as overcrowded, offensive and unhealthy. These may have been the 14 houses in King Edward Street that in 1853 were said to be occupied by 'swarms of the very vilest class'. The East Fitty Lots had similar courts, such as Marsh View Buildings, off Strand Street, which was entered through a covered passage and contained 16 houses with 58 occupants. These houses were all back-to-back and the court's eight privies faced the front of the houses close to the doors of the living rooms.[4]

A final example of poor-quality housing on the East Marsh Lots, Whitehall Yard, off King Edward Street North, had 18 houses with 77 occupants. The house walls were only half a brick thick and the privies were at the end of the court 'the whole of which is a

31 *A relic of the East Marsh Back Lots, this is Middle Court, c.1950s, with the telephone exchange in the background. It lay between Upper Burgess Street and Queen Street. The street name is still used but the site now contains the telephone exchange tower block by Ellis Way.*

32 *Part of the East Fitty Lots, which were set out for building in the early 19th century. This is Strand Street looking towards Freeman Street.*

complete swamp'. One house in the yard included the head of the household, his wife, two young daughters and four male lodgers; one of the lodgers was born in Liverpool and the rest of the occupants in Ireland. At another house lived the head of the household, his wife, six young children and four lodgers; five of the occupants were born in Ireland, four in Hull, two in Grimsby and one in Manchester. Whitehall Yard was to become particularly notorious as an area frequented by prostitutes and their clientele. In 1871, residents of four houses in the yard included 10 prostitutes. Devout Grimbarians would have been relieved to know that none of these 'ladies of the night' were born locally – five hailing from Hull, two from Boston, one each from the nearby villages of Ludborough and Utterby and one from Leicester.[5]

The borough council eventually adopted building byelaws in 1861 but they were too late to affect the development of the East Marsh Lots and East Fitty Lots. In 1872, another report on the sanitary condition of the borough criticised the rows of back-to-back houses and the many courts that could only be entered through a narrow passage.[6] Further criticism occurred in 1876 when a councillor complained of tenement property in a yard off Lower Burgess Street. He said the houses were a disgrace to the owner and that if you travelled down the yard you were likely to be either suffocated by the stench, fall into a cesspool or be hung by a clothes line.[7]

Developing the Freemen's Pastures

As the East Marsh Lots and East Fitty Lots filled with housing, the freemen's nearby East Marsh pasture became a likely area to be built over. This was anticipated by the freemen in 1849 when the Pastures Act stated that the 'borough hath of late years increased in trade and resort, and such Pastures have become very valuable for building purposes'.[8] On their appointment in 1849, members of the freemen's Pastures Committee 'deliberated upon the best scheme for rendering the pastures productive of the largest revenue and the greatest accommodation and advantage to the town'. Although turning the East Marsh pasture over to building would produce the largest revenue, the setting out of roads and drainage would be expensive and unprofitable until the building demand was sufficient to take up a large portion of land. Building was unlikely yet because the pasture was inaccessible from the dock construction area. It was cut off by railway lines on its western boundary and by the East Marsh Drain to the north. This was a wide land drain that would have to be bridged to create ready access to the new dock area before building would be economically viable.[9] In any case, cheap building land in adjacent Clee with ready access to the docks was already being turned over to housing; this area became known as New Clee.

So the freemen's interim move was to divide most of their pastures into paddocks and allotment gardens. The advantages of doing this was that they produced higher rents than pasture, while individual paddocks and gardens could be easily repossessed when needed for building. On 7 January 1850, 151 acres in the East Marsh, Haycroft and Little Field were let as paddocks and gardens, producing a total annual rental of £408. This practice continued during the 1850s. Also, a portion of the Little Field was put up for auction on building leases. The auction was largely unsuccessful but even the quarter of an acre that was taken demonstrated emphatically that building leases were a profitable way forward. It produced an annual ground rent of 2.5d. per square yard, or the gross equivalent of £50 per acre, compared with an average of less than £3 per acre from the paddocks and gardens. The comparison confirmed that, even taking into account the cost of roads and drainage, using land for building was the preferable outcome. But for the time being, the freemen had reason to be pleased with their first half-yearly dividend of 10 shillings per head, which was distributed in May 1850.[10]

Freehold or Leasehold?

During the 1850s, the expansion of the fishing industry created a further need for houses. The year 1857 saw a demand for working-class houses 'so unprecedented that there are not any to be rented neither in Grimsby nor Hull'. There was a 'great outcry' for houses near to the docks. Before building began on their East Marsh, the freemen had to decide whether to go for freehold or leasehold development. Those who were in favour of freehold development argued that if the land was sold the money received could be invested so that the freemen would have a consistent level of dividend without all the responsibility and expense of managing an estate. Their opponents argued that leasehold tenure would enable freemen of the future to benefit from any rise in the value of the land. But both sides agreed that in order to encourage rapid development, only minimal conditions should be attached to the land and that it should not be 'hampered with obnoxious restrictions'.[11]

A special meeting of the freemen was called in July 1857 to decide the issue. They were concerned that the demand for houses required 'a suitable supply of building sites on easy terms' and decided that the best way to achieve this was to lease land on 99-year leases rather than sell it.[12] The meeting also decided that a qualified surveyor should be engaged to lay out the East Marsh with roads and drainage. It is significant that this meeting was of the freemen and not of the Pastures Committee. This demonstrates the part played by the individual freemen in decision-making and also parallels the importance of the freemen in the days of the old corporation.

Planning East Marsh Building

Another special meeting of the freemen was held in September to consider the plan for the layout of the East Marsh, which had now been prepared by Louth architects James Fowler and Joseph Maughan. The latter was also the corporation's surveyor from 1856 to 1884. The plan showed a main street with streets off it at right angles.[13] The plan was agreed only after the freemen had voted to reduce the width of the main street from 60 to 50 feet, with the side streets to be 40 feet wide. This would reduce the cost of road making and also increase the amount of land available for leasing, but would also alter the appearance and spaciousness of the estate. Later in the month the Pastures Committee, acting on the instructions of the freemen, agreed on the plans of the bridge that would take the main street over the East Marsh Drain to connect with what is now called Riby Square. This was essential to opening up the land and it was decided to build it at once.[14] The bridge was on Freeman Street, approximately halfway between Kent Street and Strand Street (where there is a slight curve in Freeman Street). The drain was later culverted so there is now no visible trace of the bridge or drain.

The freemen also had to decide what type of housing to have built. There was a particular shortage of small working-class houses, known locally as 'cottages'. The East Marsh was in the right location for this sort of housing and the freemen did not want to impose restrictive conditions that could have put off potential leaseholders. Consequently, the Pastures Committee soon decided that:

> It would be very desirable to arrange the elevations in the cross and parallel streets so that working men who may have a little money may erect comfortable cottages and not have to expend their little all in making an outside show, or involve themselves in difficulties through any restrictions which might have a tendency to make them erect costly buildings in what can only be termed back streets.[15]

This line of thought is apparent in the freemen's leasing conditions. They show that most of the East Marsh was to be used for small, low-cost houses but that land in the main street was designated for better-quality houses. While a minimum of 10 shillings per square yard was required to be spent on erecting houses in the side streets, houses in the main street had to have 12 shillings per square yard spent on building them. The respective figures for the Little Field were 12 shillings and 15 shillings, as befitted its projected higher residential status.[16]

Initially, the conditions also stipulated that a minimum of 160 square yards should be apportioned to each house and its outbuildings, which could accommodate a small terrace house with a back garden. This would have been a great leap forward because, only a few years previously, 12 or more houses had been built on little more than twice this area on the East Marsh Lots and East Fitty Lots. However, it proved to be too extreme a leap for builders and potential lessees. Consequently, in 1859, it was reduced to 80 square yards on the grounds that it 'would be a great advantage to those who only want a house for themselves, and are only possessed of a limited capital'.[17]

Starting to Build

With its plans for the East Marsh layout complete by the end of 1857, and the East Marsh Drain bridged, the Pastures Committee held an auction in January 1858 of leasehold building land in the East Marsh and Little Field. The auction was a failure and was repeated a couple of months later. Only two lots were leased. Reasons for the lack of interest may have been that the reserve price for the ground rent had been fixed too high and that cheap building land nearer to the docks was still available.[18] A further possible disincentive was the initial minimum figure of 160 square yards per house which had not yet been reduced to 80 square yards.

The railway companies were making great efforts to attract smack owners to Grimsby to help get the fishing industry going, but the shortage of houses for fishermen persisted. For example, 'thirty families connected with the fishing trade were prevented from coming to reside in Grimsby for want of houses'. Such was the need that the MS&LR and the GNR eventually built 25 houses for fishermen, particularly smack owners, on land near the docks in Pollitt Street and Rowlandson Street; the houses were occupied by August 1858.[19]

The breakthrough for the freemen came about later in the year because of events in Hull. There had been disputes in the fishing trade at Hull and reports of Hull fishermen landing their catches at Grimsby because by doing so their fish could reach inland markets by the time they had sailed up river to Hull.[20] In September 1858 representatives of the Hull fishing trade, including the president of the Hull Fishing Smackowners Society, attended a meeting of the Pastures Committee to discuss leasing land in the East Marsh.

33   *Pollitt Street, which, along with Rowlandson Street, was built by the MS&LR and the GNR in 1858 to house fishermen whom they were trying to attract to the port. Seen here in July 1967.*

They wanted about 3,000 square yards near the docks. Under the Pastures Act, the land had to go to public auction. This took place in October when the Hull smack owners were reported to have leased more than 6,000 square yards and other persons about 5,000 square yards. These may have been exaggerated figures but the reserve price, 2d. per square yard, was obviously acceptable to the lessees. When the Hull smack owners were asked what they would like the street called where they had leased land, they answered that as most of them originated in Kent they would like it to be called Kent Street. More auctions and leasing followed. Most of the land in the East Marsh was leased at 2d. per square yard or slightly higher but land in advantageous positions would go for 4d. or 6d. per square yard.[21]

By November 1858, work had begun on building houses and the chairman of the Pastures Committee said the freemen had set a reasonable price on their land in order 'that they might give every industrious and persevering working man, as well as those who were in better circumstances, an opportunity of procuring a site on which to erect a dwelling house'. With building now under way, the Pastures Committee decided in 1859 that the main street on the East Marsh should be called Freeman Street. A local newspaper commented: 'This will be a noble street, fifty feet in width and we are glad that negotiations are now going on with parties desirous of taking land abutting upon it.'[22]

Development started to take off and by 1861 building leases covered over 14 acres, which increased to nearly 49 acres by 1871. The final piece of land was leased in 1872.[23] Thus, during the 14 year period 1858-72 the whole of the East Marsh pasture had been leased for building. The value of this development to the growth of the town is illustrated by the fact that during the decade 1861-71 the population of Grimsby increased by 9,177 or 83 per cent and the number of houses by 1,753 or 79 per cent. A large proportion of this growth was on the East Marsh.

Building Societies

Before any of this activity took place, builders had to acquire the necessary capital to finance house building. A significant proportion of this was raised through the medium of local building societies. They were not the modern form of large-scale 'permanent' building societies but locally established 'terminating' societies. These lasted for a pre-determined time, usually 12 to 15 years. They were formed to lease a piece of land and have a specific number of houses built on it. They raised the necessary capital by way of weekly or monthly subscriptions that were paid by shareholders to cover the cost of one or more houses. At the end of the pre-set term of years, the society came to an end, or 'terminated', and the shareholders became the owners of the houses for which they had subscribed.

The Independent Building Society was setting out land for building on the East Marsh in July 1860; by February 1861 it was intending to build 150 houses and held nearly five acres of the 14 or so acres which had been leased at that time.[24] Other societies included the Provident Building Society with 49 shareholders holding 55 plots and the Wellington Building Society, which in June 1872 arranged with builders Riggall and Hewins to build 50 houses in Wellington street, at a cost of £110 each. A month later, builder Edwin Tyson leased the final one-and-a-half acres on the East Marsh 'for a building society recently formed'.[25] The Great Grimsby Co-operative Building Society terminated in 1875 after 12 years of existence. Its shareholders acquired between them

34   *Freeman Street in the early 1900s. Although the picture shows some remaining houses, many had been converted into shops and the transformation of the street into a major shopping centre was well under way. On the right is the corner of St Andrew's Church, on the corner of Church Street.*

35   *A later view of Freeman Street, in 1963, showing the shops opposite the market. The corner of Garibaldi Street is on the left.*

114 houses located on the East Marsh in Nelson, Railway, Garibaldi and Duncombe Streets. The shareholders had each paid 4s.6d. a week for 12 years, giving an average cost of £140 per house.[26]

Some of these organisations were called building companies but the terms 'building society' and 'building company' were used rather loosely. For example, the Great Grimsby Perseverance Building Company was established in 1873 to carry on 'the usual business of a building society'.[27] In 1871, a local directory commented that:

> It is to the credit of the labouring classes of this town ... that very many of the houses in which the fishermen and other working men of Grimsby live, have been built by their co-operative endeavours, by means of Building Societies. They pay rent not to the landlord, but to themselves, and thus in a few years secure for themselves, at a cost, little, if at all, exceeding their usual rent, a local habitation of their own.[28]

Raising Capital

Capital was also needed by the freemen in order to get land ready for building by providing roads and drainage. It was up to the Pastures Committee to acquire this capital. The committee was not prepared to take money out of the estate's annual income because the freemen's dividend would have immediately gone down. We have seen that this had happened in 1858-9 and no one on the committee was eager to repeat that mistake. The only large amount of capital the freemen had was the money received from the MS&LR, but by 1865 this had all been spent or committed on roads and drainage, etc.[29] The freemen had no authority to raise mortgages so the only other option was to raise capital by selling land, which could also be criticised by the freemen because it would decrease the potential income from ground rents. However, as only minimum quantities were sold and as sales took place during a period when the freemen's dividend was high, no criticism was apparent. A block of just over three acres in the East Marsh was put up for sale but it took about seven years (1866-72) before it was all sold. It eventually raised £4,444 for roads and drainage. The block was adjacent to the market and bounded by Garibaldi, Duncombe, Freeman and Albion Streets. Later on it housed the Prince of Wales theatre (in time replaced by a cinema), the Methodist Central Hall and some very close-packed court housing (now a car park). A further seven acres were sold for £4,920 in the Haycroft during the 1870s to finance roads and drainage there. Sometimes the freemen were forced to sell land, as when the MS&LR required extra land in the Haycroft and Little Field and paid £5,800 for 10 acres by compulsory purchase in 1879.[30]

Building Control

After land had been leased for building, a surveyor was needed to supervise the building operations. Accordingly, in 1859, a part-time surveyor was appointed by the Pastures Committee. During the course of the ensuing 21 years the committee appointed and dismissed four surveyors, guaranteeing a lack of professional continuity and supervision during a time when their estate was undergoing its most radical changes. After 1880, the committee members managed without a surveyor by taking on relevant responsibilities themselves and making use of their Market Keeper. He was described in 1901 as 'really

36   *Ragged School, built in 1871 in Albert Street between Bridge Street South and Thesiger Street. Providing free basic education for the very poorest children, there were over 350 Ragged Schools in the country before they were absorbed into the Board School system. The photograph was taken immediately prior to the school's demolition in 1963, by which time it had become the Chemical Workers' Social Club.*

the surveyor for the estate generally. He has to see to drains and anything that requires attention.' They also used local surveyors as and when necessary on a fee basis.[31]

As is usual with leasehold tenure, the freemen's leases contained covenants or conditions. Some of the covenants were that substantial buildings should be built within three years of the date of the lease; that not less than 80 square yards of land should be used for every house, including its yard and outbuildings; that houses should be built up to the front line of the street; that once built, buildings should not be altered or added to without the consent of the Pastures Committee; that buildings were to be kept in good repair; and that the lessees should not permit on the premises 'any trade, manufacture or other act, matter or thing' to the damage, nuisance or annoyance of the lessors or their tenants.[32] These covenants were very much in line with those which were customary in 19th-century leases but it was how they were interpreted and enforced that helped to determine the composition and character of the freemen's estate. This was largely in the hands of the Pastures Committee and its surveyor, working within the general policy expressed by the body of freemen.

Initially, the Pastures Committee took steps to enforce the covenants but this early enthusiasm did not last and there is no indication of their consistent enforcement. The committee allowed the building of back houses and court housing, even though such housing on the East Marsh Lots and East Fitty Lots had been severely criticised in 1850.[33] The cramming of three front houses and five back houses on a plot of 382 square yards was reminiscent of the unregulated housing in the East Marsh Lots, as were the 10 houses, a fish smokehouse and a stable; all accommodated on 852 square yards of land. This unpleasant mix of houses and industry was not helped in 1871 by the fact that, 'In consequence of the Dock Company not granting building leases ... fish-curers have their principal establishments in Albion and other streets' on the East Marsh.[34] A local newspaper criticised the East Marsh building in 1873 when it said: 'The building operations in the East Marsh have been a practical experiment from which many important and useful lessons may be derived for future guidance.'[35]

The freemen's difficulty in accepting controls over building was exemplified in the attitude of John Barker who, as chairman of the Pastures Committee for 1871-85, was particularly dismissive of the need for professional overview of the estate. In 1877 after surveyor Alfred Skill had been dismissed, Barker remarked that:

> He hoped they would soon be able to do without a surveyor. Their leaseholders ... ought to be allowed some latitude. Their own interests [the freemen's] were merely in the ground rents, for which there was ample security. By not placing too stringent restrictions on their leaseholders they set an example to the landowners ... who enforce restrictions.[36]

Barker was subsequently accused of pandering to the cost-cutting and anti-regulation feelings of some of the freemen when he remarked that 'if he could avoid it they would never employ a professional man at all.'[37]

Rule by the Annual Dividend

Certainly the attitude of many of the freemen was that the job of the Pastures Committee was to provide the highest possible income from their property. Non-confrontational annual meetings meant that the freemen were happy with the current dividend, such as the one in 1872:

> From the small attendance [and] the absence of disorder ... the meeting bore a strange contrast to the stormy and excited gatherings of a few years ago ... and the committee escaped all censure and criticism whatever. This was an indication, surely, that the freemen were content with the committee, their management of the estates, and the dividends they had distributed.[38]

At the annual meeting of the freemen in 1885, the precarious nature of the Pasture Committee and its chairman's hold on office was demonstrated. There were complaints about financial matters and Barker's suggestion that they should take five shillings from the dividend to pay for the making of new roads. As a consequence, Barker was replaced by John Chapman.[39] There then followed a relatively tranquil period in the history of the Pastures Committee under Chapman's second spell as chairman, during 1885-99. Although Chapman could indulge in strident declamations when it was required, he was a more diplomatic chairman than his predecessor and emphasised their financial well-being. At the annual meeting in 1888, he met the freemen's obsession with keeping down the costs of administering their estate and emphasised how low these were. He stated that they had no liabilities, £60 in the bank, an estate worth £100,000, and an income of £3,000, but had spent only £80 on administration during the year. He said that he did not think this cost would be equalled for economy by any estate 'within the four seas'. Not surprisingly, the Pastures Committee was re-elected en bloc.[40]

The Little Field and the Haycroft

Towards the end of the 1860s the Pastures Committee was aware that all of the East Marsh would soon be taken up and that the leasing of the Little Field and the Haycroft was essential if the dividend was to keep pace with the increasing number of freemen. However, there was no immediate interest in the land there. The reason was its location. The land was on the fringe of the built-up area at a distance from the town centre and well away from the docks. This was one reason why the freemen had anticipated in 1850 that this area would be more suitable for better-class housing. A decade later a local newspaper remarked that the quagmire state of Littlefield Lane was 'almost a prohibition' to bringing the land on to the building market for 'persons desirous of providing for themselves and others comfortable and genteel residences'.[41] Interest was also muted because other large landowners had land available for leasing, for either working class or better-quality housing, which was more accessible from the town centre or dock area.

Despite its disadvantages, the freemen had no other land to bring forward, so a start was made on getting the Little Field and the Haycroft ready for building. An encouragement to building was provided by the construction of a 50-feet-wide road, Cromwell Road, as the main road of the development. There started to be some movement of the land, although with a lowering of the aspirations for the estate, when builder Edwin Tyson set out to build 48 working-class cottages. By 1881, 11 acres had been leased, still leaving over 40 acres as paddocks and gardens. There was only minimal interest in building in the Little Field and the Haycroft until the new century.[42]

The Town

So what did the town look like as it advanced into the 1870s? It was commented in the town directory for 1871 that:

> The town of Grimsby presents few attractions to the sight-seer; it is a place for business rather than a resort for pleasure. Through its whole length – a distance of about a mile and a half – and on a level with the public roads, run railway lines dividing it into two parts, the Old Town, and the New Town ... In Victoria Street [North] are some very spacious and handsome shops; one side of it is occupied principally with timber yards, mills, and wharfs, having an excellent water way and leading into the Humber.

By this time the appellation 'New Town' had been transferred to the freemen's East Marsh and its vicinity:

> The New Town is a complete network of streets; its principal one, Freeman Street, is a long, straight, and broad street, and is considered one of the finest streets in North Lincolnshire.

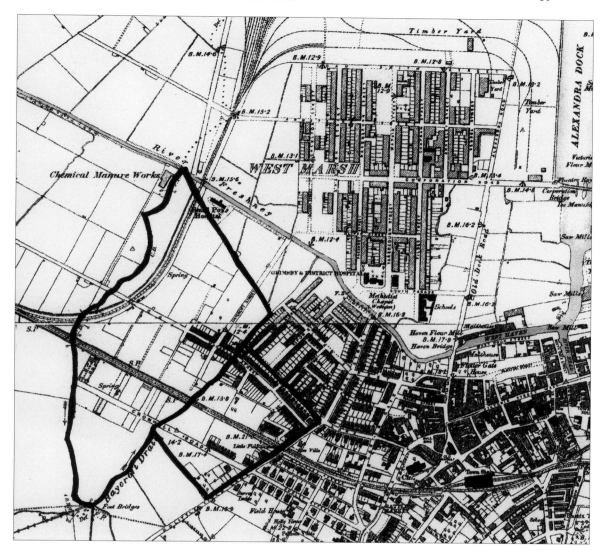

37 *The freemen's Haycroft and Little Field in 1887 (to the left within the bold lines). The partly developed West Marsh lies to the north.*

This part of the town is inhabited principally by mariners, and those connected with the fishing trade, and here it is that the great growth of Grimsby has chiefly been. During the last six years not less than 1,370 houses have been erected in the New Town, besides a large handsome Church [St Andrew's, consecrated 1870], five Chapels, a Royal Dock Hotel [built 1864-5], and a Temperance Hall [built 1871].[43]

New chapels in the East Marsh and elsewhere included the Duncombe Street Wesleyan Chapel and the Methodist Free Church in Freeman Street (both built 1868), the Spring Street Independent Chapel (1861) and the Primitive Methodist Bethel Chapel on Cleethorpe Road (1861). The Hall of Science that opened in Freeman Street in 1873 provided a secular counterbalance to the chapels and churches. The hall was available for 'Lectures on Scientific, Political, Social or Religious Subjects; Concerts, Private Quadrille

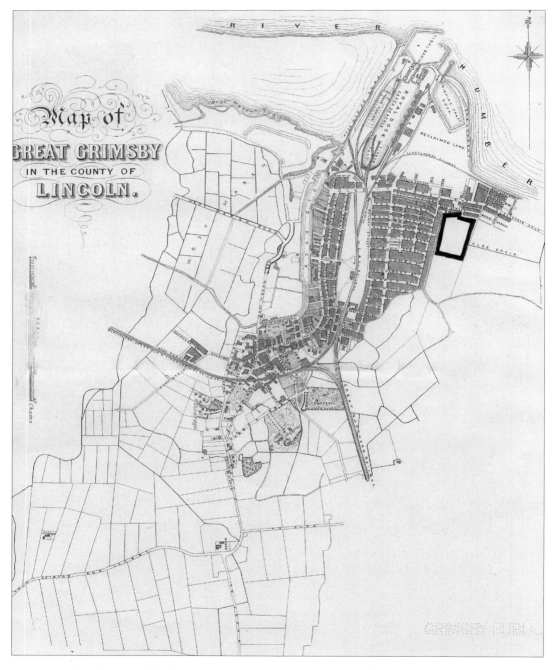

38   *Grimsby c.1870. The East Marsh pasture was now taken up with housing and railway lines. Housing that has spilled over along Cleethorpe Road into the parish of Clee may be seen in the top right-hand quadrant, where the small piece of land within the bold line is the corporation's part of the Clee Allotments. The wide and undulating East Marsh Drain prevented housing overspill lower down.*

39   *The Town Hall soon after its completion in 1863.*

Parties, Sales by Auction etc.'[44] Other new buildings in the town included the National School in the Central Market, the Spring Street Friendly Societies Hall (1864) and the Theatre Royal in Victoria Street North (built 1864, demolished 1904 and replaced by the since-demolished Palace Theatre). The town's first public hospital in modern times opened in 1865, supported by benefactors and subscribers. It was in premises on the corner of Cleethorpe Road and Tomline Street and had seven beds. Local doctors gave their services free of charge and in its first year 44 patients were treated.

One of the few major buildings of the period that has survived with its original function intact is the present Town Hall, which replaced the one built in 1780 in what became the Old Market Place. The new Town Hall was completed in 1863 as an imposing symbol of the resurgence and growing pride of the town. It provided accommodation for civic ceremonies and administration, the magistrates' court, the police and cells. It was extended, with internal alterations, in 1888.

The town had about 51 public houses in 1871, of which more than half were in the East Marsh and its environs near to the docks. In an effort to counter the drinking culture, temperance venues were opened such as the building in 1869 of the Working Men & Sailors' Free Club, on Cleethorpe Road, which was described as:

> An Iron [corrugated iron] building ... for the convenience of Sailors, Mechanics, and others, during their leisure hours, where innocent games such as draughts, bagatelle, and dominoes can be played ... there is also a ... Refreshment Bar, where simple drinks such as ginger beer, tea

and coffee can be obtained, but nothing intoxicating is allowed; there is an abundant supply of Literature, in the shape of Books, Magazines, Daily and Weekly Newspapers. The working expenses of the institute are defrayed by the donations placed in the box at the door.[45]

*   *   *

In 1872, the Pastures Committee, looking back on the decade, congratulated the freemen:

on their success in disposing of nearly the whole of their East Marsh estate at prices fair and reasonable to the purchaser, as well as being remunerative to the Enrolled Freemen. By so doing, the town generally has been greatly benefited, and more elbow room has been made for the wants of a fast increasing population. It appears to be a matter of doubt whether the town could have increased in buildings and population to the extent it has done if this plot of eligible Building Land had not been placed in the market, for apparently a stop had been placed on the Town's Extension and Improvement, by the almost fabulous prices asked for building sites. The Freemen, therefore, wisely stepped in, offered their land by public auction at a market price, and thus realised the benefits they are now enjoying – a very considerable increase of their income with a still further prospective improvement in the future.[46]

Chapter 7

Building the West Marsh

1870s

While the freemen were racing along with their development of the East Marsh, an interested observer and landowner was the municipal corporation. The pre-1835 municipal corporation had set out the first New Town on the East Marsh Lots and East Fitty Lots in 1800. Its successor, the reformed corporation, now set in motion a further phase of expansion. Before describing what action it took in expanding the built-up area, it would be helpful to look at this landowner in some detail.

The New Borough Council

The reformed corporation had a reformed borough council. As the size of the town grew, so did the size of the council, from four aldermen and 12 councillors in 1835 to 12 aldermen and 36 councillors in 1889. Occupations can be identified for 39 of the 48 members of the council in 1890. Over half were involved directly in dock industries, 15 being fishing vessel owners or fish merchants and another five had dockside businesses such as ship engineering, metalworking, timber importing and grain handling. Others were dependent on the continued prosperity of the town in their capacity as butchers, grocers and other service providers, including four publicans and three builders. These two latter occupations were always present on the council. The only professional occupations represented were two local doctors. Personal and sectional interests swayed members of the council. This was demonstrated in 1894 when those interested in the licensed trade helped to defeat moves to have a public library and were accused of ranging themselves 'against any project for adding to the intellectual well-being of the town'.[1] Another interest that was always represented was the freemen. It is not always easy to distinguish which of the members were freemen, but in 1890 at least five aldermen and two councillors were definitely freemen.[2]

Certainly during most of the later 19th century, business and sectional interests swayed council decisions to a greater extent than did political beliefs. But if the composition of the council reflected major interests in the town, this was in tune with the wishes of at least a proportion of the electorate. Comment was made in 1873 that the local 'fishermen are very independent and generally vote with a popular man or one likely to serve their own personal interests rather than from any strong political feeling'. This was borne out nearly thirty years later during the municipal elections of 1901 when, as the result of a bitter strike and lockout at the town's fish docks, fish dock representatives lost their seats on the council.[3] Although some council members fought elections under party banners, others were openly acknowledged to be representing particular interests. For example, in 1894, three candidates representing the licensed trade, one temperance candidate and one fish trade candidate joined three Labour candidates. It was possibly the presence of the Labour candidates that prompted the local Liberal newspaper to comment that municipal elections were becoming more political in character and that 'in the near future the Town Council will develop into a political assembly'. By 1895 the council included three Labour councillors but the preponderance of those council members who admitted to a party label were Liberal or Conservative.[4]

An important interest on the council, which cut across any political or sectional loyalties, was that of property. In addition to those members who were builders, a large proportion of the council had property interests. Examples are the shareholdings of Councillors Palmer and Charlton in a local building company, the property in the East Marsh held by four members and the description of Alderman George Doughty during his mayoral year as 'the largest owner of house property in the town'.[5] We shall see below that such holdings led to accusations that council members allowed their property interests to influence the council decisions that they made regarding building and sanitation controls. This situation was emphasised in the case of those councillors who leased corporation property. Those holding leases on the corporation's West Marsh estate included council members Edwin Tyson, Thomas Charlton, William Southworth and John Doughty, plus the borough surveyor Joseph Maughan who was responsible for implementing corporation building controls. There were allegations that private interests might have influenced members of the council when they and Maughan were determining the layout of the West Marsh for building in 1873.[6]

We can now begin to comprehend the wide range of sectional, business and personal interests that were represented on the council. It is not surprising, therefore, that in 1875 a visiting journalist commented on the poor quality of the town's local government, remarking that, 'Perhaps Grimsby may be a little worse than other towns in ... respect of internecine quarrelling, though my own impression is that few places could equal it'.[7]

Motivations for Developing the Estate

Despite personal interests, the reformed corporation's essential motivations for turning land over to housing were the product of its duty to the community at large. The development would provide badly needed working-class houses and would also increase the corporation's income in order to meet the needs and expectations of the increasing population. But the 210 acres of its West Marsh were in danger of being by-passed in favour of more accessible land. The only access to the marsh was in the south through the old town, whereas the demand for housing came from workers employed on the new docks to the north-east, from which the marsh was separated by the haven dock. Accordingly, the corporation applied for a private act of parliament that would permit it to bridge the dock and lay out the West Marsh for building; the act received the royal assent on 13 May 1869. The freemen opposed the act because West Marsh development could check the leasing of their East Marsh and reduce the value of their land. However, they received benefit that helped to moderate their opposition. This was the provision of the Newmarket Street footbridge over the railway lines that ran along the western flank of their East Marsh estate and limited access to it. The Corporation Bridge and the footbridge were opened in 1872 just as the last of the freemen's

40 *The first Corporation Bridge, completed in 1872 in order to open up the West Marsh for building. In the distance is the clock tower and drinking fountain in the Central Market.*

land in the East Marsh was leased.[8] As the Corporation Bridge was being constructed in 1871, it was commented that:

> The Old Dock ... [is] used chiefly for the timber trade ... [and] the side of the street adjoining the dock is occupied with timber yards, offices, saw mills, linseed oil and cake mills, and steam flour mills. On the west side until recently, it has been nearly all pasture land ... In consequence of a New Bridge now in course of erection across the dock ... the whole of the west side of the dock is being rapidly taken up for commercial purposes.[9]

Dock Extension on the West Marsh

The corporation started moves to open up the West Marsh in 1873. At the same time, as noted in chapter five, the MS&LR asked if it could purchase land on the marsh for the construction of what became the West Arm of the Alexandra Dock. The prospect of dock enlargement was certainly an attractive one for the town and its trade and employment prospects. However, as a landowner, the corporation had to consider whether cash in hand would compensate for the leasehold ground rents that the land might produce in the future. The corporation's decision-making was made easier by the fact that the land required by the MS&LR was that half of the marsh that was furthest removed from the old town and was unlikely to be required for housing for many years, if at all. Accordingly, the sale of a large amount of land would be to the best advantage of the corporation's finances, while local commerce would benefit from more dock facilities. Negotiations carried on through 1873 and, after a meeting between Sir Edward Watkin and the council, the company offered £300 an acre for over 100 acres.[10]

The sale needed the permission of the Treasury, which soon received two petitions from opponents of the transaction. The first was from a member of the council, Alderman John Wintringham, magistrate and major timber merchant. He thought the quantity of land required by the MS&LR was too large for its use but his main objection to the sale was the price of £300 per acre, which he saw as far below the actual value of the land. He also mentioned that the railway company's port manager, James Reed, was the mayor and had chaired the council meeting that had agreed to the company's request. The second petition was on the same lines and from 24 local people.[11]

The corporation's response was that the land was remote back land and the price was fair in relation to that obtained in other parts of the town. With regard to the amount of land involved, the 100 acres that would be left for building could house 20,000 people and would be sufficient for the next 20 years. This was irrespective of the hundreds of acres of building land in the town owned by other proprietors and on the market. It then argued that the dock extension was important in increasing trade and improving land values in the town. Also, it stressed that although the mayor was the port master he had offered to retire from the meeting and took no part in the proceedings, and no other members of the council were railway servants.[12]

A Treasury surveyor reported that the price offered was fair and reasonable, in view of the large amount of land involved, while the proposed docks would add value to West Marsh building land. Accordingly, the corporation ratified the sale and the company purchased 103 acres at £300 per acre.[13] The purchase money, plus interest, amounted to £32,231 and provided useful capital for the corporation. It enabled it to pay off the £4,000 mortgage that it had raised for roads and drainage on the West Marsh and to put money aside for other contingencies before investing the remaining £21,909, largely in government-consolidated stock ('consols'). This was later used for other capital expenditure such as more roads and drainage on the estate and improvements to the Town Hall.[14]

Preparing for Building

As agreement was being reached with the railway company, the shortage of working-class houses was such that a newspaper advertisement of a four-roomed house for letting received 57 responses. A local newspaper commented on 'a great outcry for houses and as spring approaches we may expect houses springing up in all directions'. It also gave the upbeat message 'that we have in our present town only the germ of the town that is to be'.[15] It was, therefore, with confidence that the corporation could set about turning its land over to housing.

The corporation appreciated that it should avoid repeating some of the worst mistakes made in the provision of local working-class housing. Its concern was highlighted with regard to about 24 acres of land known as the Clee Allotments. These were not allotments in the usual modern sense but consisted of 10 acres of land that had been 'allotted' to the corporation under the Clee parliamentary enclosure of 1842-6 to settle its manorial claims, plus 14 acres allotted to the Earl of Yarborough. These Clee Allotments lay just beyond the borough boundary and were part of the area that became known as New Clee. The corporation sold its 10 acres in 1872-3 to help finance the construction of the Corporation Bridge. The acreage lay either side of the extreme western end of Oxford Street and included the northern end of Charles Street (later renamed Hope Street). Some members of the council expressed concern about the poor-quality houses that were going up there. Others thought that, as they had sold the land freehold, the purchasers had absolute right over it, and if the council had hampered it with conditions they would not have been able to sell it.[16] Because the land was just outside the borough boundary, a local newspaper commented that an epidemic there from defective sanitation would quickly spread to Grimsby:

> Some of the houses erected in New Clee are so small and inconvenient – so unfitted for habitation – that they appear purposely designed for the breeding of disease ... one owner of some of this wretched property says that poor people do not require roomy houses; it is quite sufficient he maintains, if they have one downstairs room spacious enough for a chair or two and a table. He would be receiving his just desserts if he could be compelled to occupy one of his own hovels. The buildings ... have been erected without any road being formed, and there is as yet no drainage to any of the houses.[17]

41   *Local residents in a square off Trinity Street, c.1890s, on the heavily criticised Clee Allotments. The small boy on the right has bare feet.*

However, the corporation did not ordinarily sell its land and intended to lease the West Marsh. Its leasing conditions or covenants were similar to those of the freemen. Leases included stipulations that not less than 15 shillings per square yard was to be spent on buildings fronting streets 40 feet wide or more, and 10 shillings on other streets; not less than 80 square yards was to be used for each house, yard and outbuildings; and no trades were to be carried on which were offensive or would cause damage, nuisance or annoyance to the lessor and its tenants. By 1893 the stipulation had been added that all buildings should front on to the public street. There were no restrictions on building shops and, in the town clerk's words, 'you can build shops or what you like'.[18]

The West Marsh layout was very much on the lines of the freemen's East Marsh with a main street of better-quality houses and side streets comprising terraces of small working-class 'cottages'. This was not surprising because Joseph Maughan, who, with James Fowler, drew up the street layout for the East Marsh, drew up the plan. However, it was hoped to avoid some of the mistakes that had been made in developing the East Marsh. In addition to learning from the freemen's experience, there was a growing appreciation of the importance of public health and in 1872 the corporation adopted some provisions of the 1872 Public Health Act. A local newspaper commented that:

> It is to be hoped that in the laying out of the streets [of the West Marsh] and the allotment of the land greater attention will be paid to ... the class of houses to be built, their efficient drainage, their strength of construction, their uniformity of height and design, the supply of water, and other matters of detail, than was the case on the Freemen's estate.[19]

42   *The West Marsh in 1969, showing Corporation Road at the junction with Rendel Street.*

Building Society Domination

Before any land was leased, there was disagreement between the corporation and the terminating building societies. The societies wanted the land auctioned in large blocks. In February 1873 the Victoria Building Society wanted land on which to build 100 houses and a month later it was reported that societies had applied for 30 acres. However, the corporation wanted land to be leased in smaller blocks. A compromise was reached with lots ranging from 350 to 10,000 square yards. Some believed that councillors had personal reasons for making smaller lots available and, as we have seen, some did lease land personally on the marsh.[20] The societies threatened to boycott the West Marsh if their demands were not met:

> If you can oblige us we shall be glad; if not we shall go elsewhere for the land. We can get it at 2d. a yard [elsewhere]. If we hang together as societies, which we probably shall, you will not let the land ... It is no use to us to have a bit here and a bit there.[21]

Despite the threats, three societies took part in the first auction and between them took 14 of the 23 acres that were leased. The average ground rent bid at this first sale was just over 2.5d. a square yard. By 1877 nearly 50 acres had been leased. The first decade of development was very successful and, in 1883, the corporation had an estate of 764 leasehold properties, including 703 houses and 41 house-shops. The societies certainly dominated the early development of the marsh and by 1883 there were eight operating on the estate. Between them they held 536 of the 703 houses that had been built.[22]

The estate was set out in a grid-iron street layout of basic terraced working-class houses which did not display the undesirable aspects of the freemen's East Marsh, such as courts, back housing or back-to-backs. The estate also included public or community

43 *Grimsby Hospital on the West Marsh, built in 1877 and superseded by the Diana, Princess of Wales hospital in 1983.*

buildings with a mission church, several mission chapels, a board school and the town's new hospital, plus a small isolation hospital that was situated on the extreme western edge of the estate. There was good reason why the corporation should have been very satisfied with its operations in the West Marsh. It had succeeded financially in the venture and within five years had increased its total estate rental income by 50 per cent, from £2,006 in 1871 to £3,022 in 1875.[23]

Land for Public Amenities

By leasing its land the corporation received a sizeable annual income that helped to finance public services. But as a local authority it was also expected to use its land for public amenities, which produced no income. Therefore, it had to strike a balance between these two conflicting demands on its land. It sometimes took on the role of public benefactor and obtained permission from the Treasury to lease land to public bodies at nominal rents. One instance regarded the town's hospital provision. An appeal was launched to fund a replacement for the Cleethorpe Road premises and a new purpose-built hospital was opened on the West Marsh in 1877. The site was leased from the corporation, subject to the payment of an annual peppercorn rent of one shilling. A similar instance regarded the South Parade Board School, built in the West Marsh in 1879.

A recurring issue for the corporation during 1875-7 was the provision of land for public recreation. It had obtained powers in its improvement act of 1869 to use part of the West Marsh for a public park and considered that up to 25 acres might be needed. Opinions both inside and outside the council were divided on account of the financial implications. These were threefold: loss of potential ground rents; the capital cost of forming the park;

and the cost of its annual maintenance. Eventually, the corporation lowered its ambitions and proposed a small 'boulevard', or linear park, by the River Freshney on its West Marsh land. Supporters of the need for a park pointed to the bad example of the freemen's East Marsh, where all the land had been built on 'and there was nothing for the working classes to look upon'. But support was patchy and opponents argued that there were more important matters to spend money on, such as improved sanitation. Others maintained that a park was not needed because of the proximity of fields and seashore.[24] The purchase of half of the West Marsh by the railway company also gave opponents the excuse that the corporation could no longer spare land for a park. So no immediate action was taken on the proposal for a 'boulevard' park.

In contrast to its lack of commitment to using its land for public recreation, the corporation used its East End Closes as a reservoir of land for other public or public-related purposes. It is probable that this came about because of the location of the land and the force of circumstances. When the closes were leased for grazing in 1841, they comprised 33 acres. Over five acres were sold later to the ELR for the final stretch of its line into Grimsby. In 1855, eight-and-a-half acres became the town cemetery. In the 1860s, land was taken for the new Town Hall and freemen's schools and six acres were sold to the Grimsby Gas Company for a new gasworks.[25] Therefore, by the time that the corporation was considering entering into leasing land for housing, only 14 or so acres remained, leased as paddocks or gardens and with restricted access.

Estate Administration

Two officers of the corporation would be instrumental in the administration of the estate, namely the town clerk and the borough surveyor – both of whom we have already met. They ran extensive private practices and acted in a part-time capacity for the corporation. The town clerk, solicitor William Grange, held the post from 1861 until his death in office in 1913. On his 87th birthday in 1908, a local newspaper described him as working at his solicitor's office until 5.30 p.m. and then attending evening committee meetings: 'He is acquainted at first hand with every piece of corporation work and knows its details. Everybody takes a rest but the town clerk.' His unwearying appetite for work, his local knowledge, his understanding of law and the work of the corporation, his length of service and his domination of the corporation's administration resulted in the borough council making him an honorary freeman of the borough. This was 'in recognition of valuable and distinguished service rendered by him to the borough'.[26] He was also a freeman by birth and had a strong allegiance to the freemen, which raised comments questioning his loyalty to the corporation. This uneasy situation was exacerbated by the stipulation in the freemen's Pastures Act of 1849 that the town clerk must also serve as clerk to the freemen.

The borough surveyor was the officer more immediately involved with the estate. Joseph Maughan held the post for 28 years, 1856-84. He was also surveyor to the local commission of sewers and acted for other landowners, including the Earl of Yarborough and Edward Heneage. He planned the street layout of the West Marsh and, with James Fowler of Louth, the East Marsh. He was involved in the planning or supervision of many other significant local developments, including the town's first municipal cemetery, the Old Market, the Central Market, the Freeman Street Market and so on. In the 1870s the corporation became dissatisfied with his lack of attention to his work and he was given notice to leave his post in October 1876. A month later this was rescinded and he was allowed to continue as surveyor but told to relinquish some of his outside work and devote all his time to his corporation duties. He was accused by councillors of superintending new roads for Yarborough and Heneage when he should have been carrying out his municipal duties, but he was also criticised frequently by Heneage for dilatory behaviour. Criticism surfaced again in 1884 when the corporation accused him of drinking and dereliction of duty and threatened him with dismissal. Instead, he was made consulting engineer to the corporation at a salary of £100 per annum and the corporation advertised for a full-time surveyor at an annual salary of £200, 'to devote the whole of his time to the duties of his office'. John Buchan of Plymouth was appointed full-time borough surveyor in 1884.[27]

Lack of Municipal Control

In contrast with earlier times, there was now a greater appreciation nationally of the need to provide healthy surroundings and well-built housing for the working class. The laws

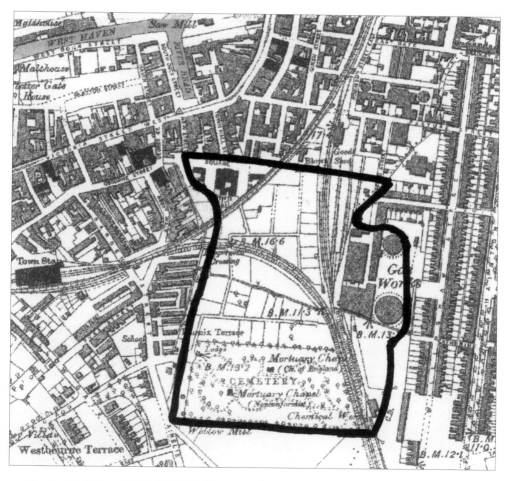

44 *East End Closes (within the bold line) in 1887. They lay to the east of Doughty Road and stretched between (and included) the Town Hall Square and the Town Hall in the north and the site of the old municipal cemetery in the south.*

relating to public health were revised and codified in the Public Health Act of 1875, and in 1877 the Local Government Board produced new model building byelaws. By the end of the 1880s most authorities had byelaws that conformed to this new national model. In view of its reluctance in the 1850s to be a Local Health Board, it is not surprising that Grimsby was not among these enlightened authorities. It continued to operate under its outdated 1861 byelaws and it was not until 1892 that it adopted more comprehensive and detailed building byelaws. The corporation's reluctance to take a more positive stance in improving local control of building was reinforced by its dual role as a land developer and local authority. Having council members who had trade and building interests compounded this. As both land developer and local authority, the corporation was acting in two separate categories on its own estate. It had to develop the land to its own best financial advantage and yet dispassionately ensure that local government controls were properly applied. Predictably, it was accused of not fulfilling its public duties. In particular, there were many criticisms of the roads and footpaths on the West Marsh and in 1889 one councillor called it the most neglected part of the town.[28]

The corporation was also lax in applying building controls and allowed builders to ignore the building byelaws. In 1878 it did take legal action against breaches of the building regulations and byelaws. The ineffectual result of the court proceedings was that five persons were fined 12 shillings each by the magistrates. Maughan as good as admitted laxity when he told the bench that the corporation intended to enforce the byelaws strictly in future. A local newspaper commented: 'There is thus a reasonable prospect that sanitary regulations which in too many cases have been totally disregarded in the past, will receive due consideration in the construction of new buildings.' However, the corporation's lack of control persisted and in 1887 some councillors argued, unsuccessfully, for the appointment of a building inspector.[29]

Other Development

While the freemen and the corporation had been leasing their extensive estates, limited building had been taking place in the old town. Some of this involved replacing existing buildings but most construction was on vacant land held by the Yarborough and Tennyson families and others. The main Yarborough undertaking was to build housing on their land lying between the River Freshney and Pelham Road. The building is in two distinctive parts. North of Chantry Lane is terraced housing, which can be distinguished by such unsurprising street names as Lord Street and Earl Street. South of Chantry Lane the area includes Dudley Street and was used mainly for detached and semi-detached villas.

George Tennyson's Grimsby land was now held by his grandson, Frederick Tennyson (1807-98). He was an absentee landlord who spent most of his adult life in Italy and Jersey, where he pursued his, mainly artistic, interests. His younger brother was the future Poet Laureate Lord Alfred Tennyson and his father was Dr George Clayton Tennyson (1778-1831) who was absentee Vicar of Grimsby during 1815-31. The land that Frederick inherited in Grimsby (and Cleethorpes) was dispersed in fairly small holdings and the 1870s saw quite a lot of leasehold housebuilding on his vacant land in the area of the medieval town. Garden Street, Abbey Walk and Peppercorn Walk (by the present Doughty Road) were leased for housing. Infilling or redevelopment of individual plots took place in Bethlehem Street, Brewery Street, Osborne Street and West and South St Mary's Gate. Over in Bargate six detached or semi-detached villas were built and

45 *The site of Doughty Road, looking towards the site of the present Central Library. Doughty Road and the underpass were built in 1895. To the left is Peppercorn Walk.*

Abbey Road saw the leasing of land for the well-known 'Spectacle Row' of large terraced houses. More Tennyson leasing took place in the town centre in the 1880s. Clayton Street was set out and built up and houses were also built on the north side of Sanctuary Lane. Quite a lot of building was carried out in Cartergate, New Cartergate, Crescent Street and Chantry Lane, plus a few houses in Flottergate and limited infilling in Osborne Street, Haven Street and Victoria Street.[30]

Another local landowner was 'Colonel' George Tomline (1813-99), who was born at nearby Riby Grove. Because of his service with the Lincolnshire volunteer militia, Tomline retained the honorary title of Colonel and was reputed to be the wealthiest commoner in the country. He had strong ancestral family connections with Suffolk and for most of his life he lived at his country seat, Orwell

46 *Clarence Terrace in Abbey Road in the 1870s, better known as Spectacle Row from the shape of the dormer windows. Is it building or demolition taking place in the foreground?*

47   *Better-quality terraced housing. St James' Terrace in Bargate, c.1870.*

Park in Suffolk, or his London mansion overlooking the Mall. He inherited considerable property and purchased much more, particularly in Suffolk, and became the second largest landowner in that county, holding 18,479 acres. His Riby Grove estate of 8,439 acres produced an annual rental of £11,534. He served in parliament for 29 years, representing Grimsby during 1868-74. His greatest practical achievements were in Suffolk during 1877-86 where he financed the construction of a railway from Ipswich to the coast, had a dock constructed and thereby set in motion the growth of the modern port and resort of Felixstowe. His land in Grimsby consisted of the old Ropery site, which he purchased for £20,000. He set out its 29 acres in 1861 for developing on 99-year leases.[31] Building took place on its Cleethorpe Road frontage and on Riby Street, Orwell Street, Tomline Street, and three streets named after Suffolk villages where he had land and property, i.e. Nacton, Kesgrave and Levington Streets.

Other building in the town during the 1870s included several new churches and chapels to cater for the increasing population and the new housing developments. These included the Wesleyan Victoria Chapel on Cleethorpe Road (1871), the Garibaldi Street Primitive Methodist Chapel (1876), the Baptist Chapel in Freeman Street (1871), the Victoria Street Baptist Tabernacle (1878) and the St Barnabas (corrugated iron) Mission Church in King Edward Street North (1874). Dock trade led to the building of the Customs House in Cleethorpe Road (1874) and the Grimsby Fisherlad's Institute in Orwell Street (1879-80). The building of the Masonic Hall in Osborne Street (1875) emphasised the strength of local freemasonry. The Central Market was embellished with a clock tower and drinking fountain, which was given by Edward Bannister in 1870 during his mayoral year. In accordance with the requirements of the 1870 education act, a Grimsby School Board was appointed in 1874 and the town's first Board School was built on Heneage land just outside the borough boundary at Holme Hill and opened in 1877.

Chapter 8

Building Clee and Weelsby
1860s-1880s

Despite the extensive housebuilding on the East and West Marsh, it was not sufficient to meet the ever-increasing demand for housing within striking distance of the docks. There was still a lot of undeveloped land in the town but most of it was too far from the docks, such as the hundreds of acres owned by the Earl of Yarborough in the south of the borough. The only easily accessible land lay to the east of Grimsby, outside the borough boundary in the parish of Clee. Two landowners held most of this land. We shall see how the development of their land altered the shape of Grimsby and had other major repercussions on the town.

Landowners

The largest landowner in Clee was Alexander Grant-Thorold (1820-1908). Originally Alexander Grant, he adopted the surname Grant-Thorold in 1864 on inheriting the estate of his childless uncle, Richard Thorold. Thereupon, he lived locally at Weelsby House, became a Justice of the Peace and was High Sheriff of Lincolnshire in 1870. He lived in London from 1890. The Thorold family were an ancient family of country gentry. Their main presence was in south Lincolnshire but there were also long-standing connections with north-eastern Lincolnshire. Some members of the family had been freemen of Grimsby in times past and had served as aldermen and mayors of the borough. The estate inherited by Grant-Thorold in 1864 comprised 1,628 acres of which 1,212 acres were in Clee, Cleethorpes and Weelsby.

Coincidentally, the other prominent landowner in Clee also inherited his estate in 1864. He was Edward (later Lord) Heneage (1840-1922) who came into the family estate on the death of his father George Heneage. He became the Grimsby Member of Parliament during the 15 years 1880-95, except for a short break in 1892-3. He began his political career as a Liberal but became a Unionist after disagreeing with Gladstone's policy on Irish Home Rule in 1886. He was granted a peerage in 1896 following his election defeat of 1895. Heneage was a member of an important gentry family and inherited 10,761 acres. With the exception of 1,500 acres in Grimsby and Clee, most of his land lay in the neighbourhood of the family seat at Hainton in the Lincolnshire Wolds. The Heneage family had been associated with Grimsby since the 15th century as Members of Parliament, High Stewards and landowners. The bulk of their Grimsby and Clee acreage was obtained after the dissolution of the monasteries in the 1530s when Sir Thomas

48   *Alexander William Grant-Thorold c.1870. As the largest landowner in the parish of Clee (which adjoined Grimsby) he determined the nature of a large area of Grimsby.*

49   *Edward Heneage pictured in 1874. He was the most influential of the private landowners in shaping the character of much of Grimsby.*

Heneage (1480-1553), who was one of Henry VIII's inner circle of courtiers, acquired the lands of Wellow Abbey. Such was Sir Thomas's status in court that he was one of only four or five witnesses to the secret marriage of the King to Anne Boleyn in 1533. Sir Thomas held the influential court position of Groom of the Stool. When we consider the following description of one of his court duties, it could be said that he richly deserved his acquisition of the local land:

> Henry VIII had a toilet, known as a close stool. The Groom of the Stool was one of the most senior household officers. He was responsible for this richly upholstered piece of furniture and had to attend Henry whenever he used it. Such close personal contact with the King gave the Groom real political power.[1]

Hopefully, Sir Thomas would have been able to delegate to an ambitious junior aide his attendances at these royal command performances. In more recent times his intriguing court position has masqueraded under the sanitised title of Groom of the Stole.

Building New Clee

Grant-Thorold was the first of our two Clee owners to benefit from Grimsby's rapid growth. The borough's eastern boundary ran north-south down what is now Humber Street and then crossed Cleethorpe Road to run between Albion Street (which was in Grimsby) and Victor Street (which was in Clee). Cleethorpe Road gave convenient access to the nearby dock area from the northern part of Clee. Accordingly, by the mid-1860s building was taking place in Clee either side of Cleethorpe Road on land mostly owned by Grant-Thorold. By 1885 an extensive gridiron development of largely working-class housing lay between the Grimsby boundary and the Cleethorpes boundary at Park Street. The area became known as New Clee. Subsequent development of Grant-Thorold land was delayed because of a dispute with Heneage. Consequently, most of this chapter will be concerned with the Heneage estate. The dispute and its consequences are described in chapter ten.

Building Weelsby

The Heneage land in Clee lay to the south of Grant-Thorold's and was mainly in the area known as Weelsby. We have seen that in 1849 Edward's father, George Heneage, obtained permission under the Pastures Act to bridge the East Marsh Drain where it crossed Pasture Street (near the junction with the present Willingham Street). This gave Grimsby residents access to his land. Thereupon, in response to demand from Grimsby, he divided fields into paddocks and gardens, which produced higher rents than farm land. In 1860, he was hoping to let land at Holme Hill for building.[2] However, the demand was for building land that was convenient for the docks and he was denied access to this lucrative market because the East Marsh Drain also prevented access into Freeman Street and the docks. George died in 1864 and by 1870 Edward had purchased from the freemen the right of road access into their East Marsh. This would enable him to bridge the East Marsh Drain at what is now Hainton Square, giving him access to Freeman Street. He

50 *Memorial in Hainton Church to Sir Thomas Heneage and his wife and daughter. He laid the foundations of the Heneage family's vast Grimsby estate when he acquired the lands of the Wellow Abbey after the dissolution of the monasteries in the 1530s.*

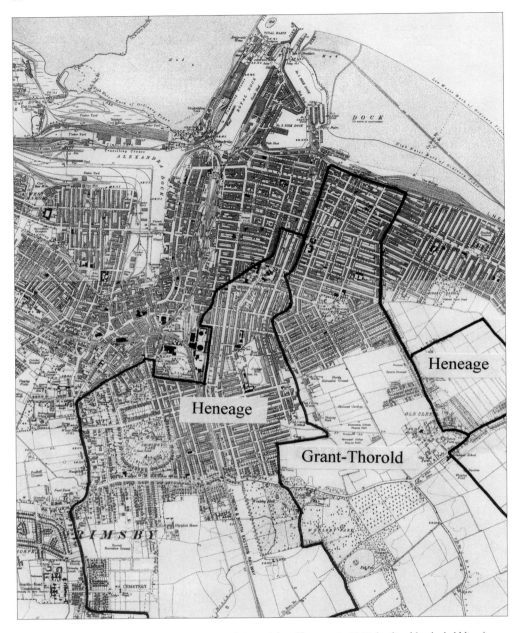

51   *The northern portions of the Heneage and Grant-Thorold estates in 1887 (outlined by the bold lines).*

could then continue Freeman Street to the south as Hainton Street (later Avenue) and link it to Pasture Street. This would open up his land for building by giving him access to both the dock area and the old town. Also, it would benefit the freemen by providing a good road between their East Marsh and the old town.[3]

So in 1870 Heneage invited tenders for the construction of bridges over the drain to give access to the East Marsh at what are now Hainton Square, Albion Street and Wellington Street.[4] It is impossible to overestimate the importance of Heneage's bridging of the drain

52   *From fields to streets in Weelsby, 1847-75.*

1847 – Part of Heneage's Weelsby land set out as farmland and separated from the freemen's East Marsh pasture by the East Marsh Drain. Pasture Street stops at the drain.

1868 – East Marsh Drain now bridged at Pasture Street, which enabled farmland to be divided into gardens (speckled) and paddocks, producing higher rents. Freemen's East Marsh now set out with streets but overspill onto Heneage land prevented by East Marsh Drain.

1875 – East Marsh Drain now bridged at Hainton Square, Wellington Street and Albion Street, enabling Heneage land to be set out with streets. Higher income now produced from building leases.

at Hainton Square and the effect it would have on the shape of the town. He emphasised the measure of his achievement when in 1872 he was asked to speak at the opening of the Corporation Bridge. Referring to the euphoria at the opening of the corporation's bridge, he said: 'I feel that I have provided a useful little bridge in Freeman Street but which has not had all the row about it that this has had, and yet I should not at all be surprised if my bridge were to prove the more useful.'[5]

It had certainly opened up his extensive Weelsby estate for building and he was now nicely poised to take advantage of building demand from both the 'old' and 'new' parts of the borough.

Planning for Change

Heneage took a great deal of personal interest in developing his Grimsby and Weelsby land but he lived at Hainton and needed people in Grimsby to advise him and carry out his instructions. Accordingly, he appointed Joseph Maughan as his local surveyor and Grimsby solicitor John Wintringham as his local agent. Wintringham was in partnership with our old friend William Grange but was not a freeman. The firm of Grange and Wintringham was already the Heneage family's local solicitors. Wintringham came from an important local family and was Liberal in politics. Heneage had done well in appointing as his local agent an influential solicitor who had important local connections and who shared his Liberal political beliefs.

As Heneage turned land over to housing, he tried to ensure that building land was available in the right quantity, at the right time, without leaving it unproductive. He achieved this by following the practice employed by his father and the freemen. This was to carve up land in potential building areas into temporary paddocks and gardens. An acre of land would contain six to eight gardens, which met an urban need for garden land. Paddocks ranged between two and six acres and were used for grazing horses and other livestock. In 1873 a local newspaper commented on the great demand for grazing land, 'which is now exceedingly scarce ... and if other neighbouring landowners were to adopt a similar course to that Mr Heneage is about taking they would not only confer a boon to Grimsby but would also largely augment their rent-rolls'.[6]

Heneage's paddocks and gardens were let on six-month tenancies and while meeting local needs they also produced much higher rents than farmland. In 1872, the annual rent of nine acres converted to paddocks was increased from £12 to £28. But more significantly, the practice increased the readiness of land for building. In 1877 Heneage urged Wintringham to take steps to let building land so that they could see what 'fresh paddocks we shall require next spring'.[7]

Although gardens and paddocks produced higher rents, the biggest gains were made when land was turned over to building. We have seen that the corporation and the freemen achieved this by leasing out their land on 99-year building leases. That Heneage followed suit is not surprising. In landed families the current head of the family was regarded as a temporary custodian charged with keeping the estate intact for passing on to succeeding generations; consequently, land was leased and only sold when absolutely essential. So Heneage leased out his land on 99-year building leases on the payment of annual ground rents, mostly at the local norm of about 2d. per square yard. But before building he had to set out roads and drainage. By 1877 his expenditure on this was £9,615 and a further estimated £10,000 would be needed to set out side streets and extend the major roads. During 1868-72, he had raised £26,682, mainly by selling about thirty acres on the western fringe of his Grimsby land (along Bargate and Abbey Road). Despite these sales he still needed to raise a mortgage in 1877 to pay for the next phase of road works in Weelsby.[8]

Building Societies Again

Once the estate was ready for building, the terminating building societies were much in evidence. In 1873, a local newspaper reported on, 'A Building Society mania in Grimsby, organisations of such associations being on foot for the erection of houses in all parts of the town ... the scarcity of houses ... is undoubtedly giving an impetus to the promotion of these societies'.[9]

Heneage stated in 1877 that one of the reasons Weelsby was a success was that he had 'cultivated a connection with the Building Societies'. In 1876, 15 terminating societies paid half of the Weelsby annual ground rents.[10] The prevalence of the societies is emphasised in the Grimsby directory for 1880, which lists forty-four. Their names show associations with a wide range of interests. Patriotism is represented by the Victoria, the Albert, the Nelson and the Wellington Societies; politics by the Gladstone Society; temperance by the Good Templars' Company; optimism by the Hopeful Company; integrity by the Good Intent Society; fatalism by the Phoenix Society; local industry by the aptly named Skipper and His Mate Building Company and doggedness by the Perseverance Society (which was also referred to as a 'company').[11] The names of the societies add a touch of flamboyance to what are not the most exciting institutions but such colour was too good to last and as they 'terminated' the more prosaic 'permanent' building societies became the norm, such as the mundanely named Great Grimsby and North Lincolnshire Permanent Building Society.

A high level of building was maintained in Weelsby during the 1870s and 1880s. This was helped in 1881 with the construction, by the Provincial tram company of Portsmouth, of a horse-drawn tramway system. The route commenced in Bargate at Welholme Road and ran through the Old Market Place and then along Victoria Street and Cleethorpe Road to the Park Street boundary. A spur ran off at Riby Square down Freeman Street and Hainton Street as far as Tasburgh Street, which at that time marked the southern limit of the Weelsby built-up area. This provision of cheap public transport encouraged the development of such outlying areas by enabling people to travel greater distances to work, and thereby making Weelsby a more convenient place in which to live.

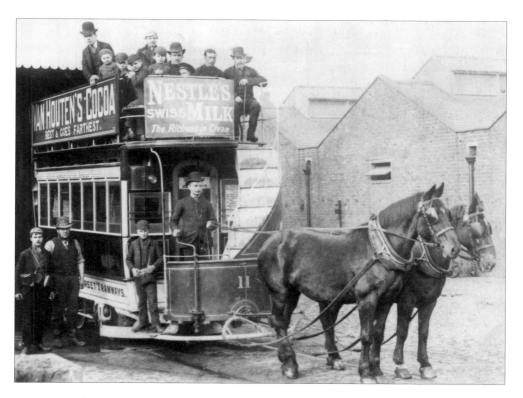

53 *Grimsby horse-drawn tram c.1890. These trams ran from 1880 to 1901, when the service was electrified.*

A Place to Live

In previous chapters we have seen the inadequate way in which the corporation and the freemen developed and managed their estates. Heneage had a much more conscientious and responsible attitude. This is shown in his self-congratulatory comment on his Weelsby estate in 1884:

> Good wide roads have been laid down and everything requisite done to improve the sanitary condition of the District. Convenient sites have been allotted for Schools and Places of Religious Worship, and the various Building Societies and Individual Leaseholders have willingly entered into such covenants as would protect the neighbourhood against those evils from which other portions of the town too notoriously suffer; whilst the character of the estate stands out conspicuously in the comparatively small yearly average of offences coming before the Magistrates or Assizes.[12]

He influenced and maintained the standards of his estate by the usual covenants in his leases that we have seen employed by the corporation and freemen. In contrast with those bodies, his covenants were enforced and he had an additional covenant forbidding the sale of intoxicating liquor. This was firmly applied and in 1895 his estate had no public houses and only two beer retailers, which were in Victor Street where the estate merged into the Clee Allotments. This contrasted sharply with the adjacent East Marsh, which, at that time, had 38 public houses and 58 beer retailers. Very few industrial or commercial premises were permitted. Shops were allowed in limited numbers and mainly in Hainton Street, in line with its importance as the main thoroughfare.[13]

He also determined the character of his estate by creating different areas for different types of residents. His land to the north (including Charles Street, Victor Street and Guildford Street) was nearest to the docks and also merged into the poor housing of the Clee Allotments, so he had small working-class terraced houses built here. The residents were largely fishermen, tradesmen and labourers. South of this area was Holme Hill, which eventually contained the Holme Hill Board School, St Mary's Roman Catholic Church, the Sir Moses Montefiore Synagogue, St Luke's Anglican Church and the offices of the Local Board of Health. These provided a 'sanitary corridor' of public buildings that separated the working-class housing from an area of detached and semi-detached villas where lived mainly employers, merchants and professional people. This area included Eleanor Street and the parts of Hainton Street and Heneage Street (later Road) north of Pasture Street. South of Pasture Street, there were good-sized terraced houses lived in by a preponderance of clerks, shopkeepers and tradesmen. Willingham Street, with its smaller houses, mainly accommodated clerical workers, tradesmen, railwaymen, fishermen and labourers.[14]

Heneage achieved this 'social engineering' by stipulating the annual rent that each house would bring in if rented out. For example, when he sold land in 1872-3 to raise capital, he selected land in Grimsby that was far from the docks and along Bargate and Abbey Road. He indicated that it would be sold freehold for 'Villa Residences'. Local press comment was that, 'Not only would such villas be an ornamental attraction to the principal highway entrance to our town, but, affording as they would the comparative quietitude of a country residence with close proximity to the town; they would be decidedly appropriate for merchants and others engaged in business here.'[15]

Heneage stipulated that 'no dwelling house of less that £25 per annum to be erected' on lots along Bargate and Welholme Avenue. Lots on Abbey Road were for houses of not less than £12 rental per annum, while houses to be built in the Duchess Street area were to be worth not less than £9 rental per annum. By such means he created separate areas of higher and lower quality houses and of corresponding social composition. A wider sample of houses in Weelsby reveals that, in 1886, a sizeable minority (12 per cent) were worth at least £20 per annum in rent and could be regarded as villas; the majority (84 per cent) were in the middle annual rent band of £10-£19 and only a negligible number (four per cent) were below £10. This compares well with the freehold Clee Allotments poor-quality housing, where annual rental values as low as £5 were common.[16]

By Victorian standards most of his tenants lived in pleasant surroundings. Such was the pride of Hainton Street residents that in 1885 they raised a public subscription to plant trees in the street; Heneage contributed £50. The reasons they gave were that it would increase the value of their property and make the street a model one. Its name was later changed to 'Avenue'. In 1889 Heneage stated that he looked with 'considerable pride at the healthy and airy dwelling places of the artisan and wage-earning classes on my estate'.[17] In general, Heneage had created a place to live that was acceptable by any reasonable standards. It had good-quality housing and sufficient amenities to provide the basis for a secure and comfortable life. This had been achieved largely because of Heneage's self-imposed standards and controls.

The estate also served as a better-quality residential area for those who were 'on the way up' either financially or socially. For example, between 1871 and 1881 fish merchant George Chamberlain moved from Church Street on the East Marsh to Hainton Square; fish salesman George Alward moved from Cleethorpe Road to Hainton Street by which time he had become a smack owner; builder Joseph Hewins moved from Freeman Street to Hainton Street, where he had now become a 'Builder and Contractor'; brickmaker Joseph Loughton moved from Duncombe Street to live in Eleanor Street as another 'Builder and Contractor'; and police constable James Frow of East Marsh Street had been promoted to police sergeant by the time he moved to Heneage Street.[18]

54 *Better-quality housing on the Heneage estate on tree-lined Hainton Avenue. The trolley bus service began in 1926.*

People's Park

With regard to land for recreation, and in view of the borough council's reluctance to provide a park, John Wintringham opened up to the public the grounds of his house off Abbey Road at advertised times during the 1870s. Heneage was elected Grimsby's Member of Parliament in 1880 and in the following year offered the council a gift of 27 acres for a park. In reporting Heneage's offer, a local newspaper commented on the need for a park: 'There is no place in Grimsby or the neighbourhood where the public can resort at will in any great numbers for the purpose of pleasure and recreation.' The intransigent opposite opinion continued to be expressed. Alderman Dr Keetley remarked that, 'A park was no more needed in Grimsby than in Switzerland.' Presumably he was in the visually challenged position of seeing no difference between the scenery of the Alps and that of Grimsby.[19] In the event, Heneage's offer was accepted and the corporation used £6,000 of its consols in transforming the land into People's Park, which opened in 1883. Heneage was accused, mainly by political opponents, of giving the land for political or financial reasons. Politically, his gift could only serve him well. Financially, he stood to gain from increased property values because he reserved the land around the park for villa residences. People's Park became the attractive centrepiece of his principal area of villa development.

55 *People's Park fountain, postcard postmarked 1912.*

56 *People's Park, the centrepiece of Edward Heneage's villa development in Wellow.*

Leasehold Enfranchisement

Because of the local practice of leasing land rather than selling it freehold, Grimsby was cited in parliamentary committees in the 1880s as a leasehold town. This arose during national controversy regarding the rights and wrongs of the leasehold system.[20] Two of our landowners, Edward Heneage and the municipal corporation, became involved in the controversy. One area of contention was to what extent leaseholders (lessees) should have the right to purchase the freehold of their property from landowners (lessors). This process of purchasing the freehold of a leasehold property is known as enfranchisement.

Both the corporation and the freemen had tried to enfranchise some of their leaseholds to their lessees in the 1870s for short-term financial reasons. Both requests were denied by the Treasury on the grounds that it was in neither body's long-term interests.[21] The only times when the corporation and freemen were allowed to enfranchise leases was in the case of the sites of religious buildings and it was a general practice locally for the large landowners to permit religious bodies to purchase the freehold of their church or chapel site.[22]

During the 1880s criticism was directed at landowners such as Heneage who reaped vast gains in 'unearned' income from leasehold building land. Accordingly in 1883 the national Leaseholds Enfranchisement Association was formed. Its object was to promote a Leaseholds Enfranchisement Bill under which urban leaseholders would have the right to purchase the freehold of their property. Grimsby was stated to have 80 per cent of its property held on lease compared with the largely freehold land of Louth, Lincoln and Hull. Not surprisingly, therefore, a Grimsby branch of the association was formed in October of the same year. It criticised non-resident landlords for getting high ground rents and insisting on onerous covenants, restricting the availability of land and generally holding back commerce and enterprise.[23]

Heneage spoke against the enfranchisement bill in parliament in 1883 and emphasised that the leasehold system was to the great advantage of the working class who, with the aid of building societies, could become owners of their own homes. The bill was defeated but even so in the following year Heneage offered to enfranchise leaseholds in Weelsby at 25-years' purchase of the ground rent. For example, someone paying £4 a year ground rent could purchase the freehold of their house for 25 times this amount – £100. This offer pleased the Leaseholds Enfranchisement Association, which wrote in 1885 that his arrangements 'reflect the highest credit upon all concerned'. Despite this commendation, few leaseholders took advantage of the offer. Twenty-six did so in 1885 but the ensuing six years saw only another 18 in total.[24]

The lack of interest is not surprising. The leasehold system had worked successfully locally in enabling a large quantity of housing to be built quickly. Ground rents were low and builders did not have to raise capital in order to purchase sites. Supporters of leasehold, such as Councillor Tyson, a builder of small working-class houses, argued that leasehold had been a great benefit for Grimsby. Freehold land could not be sold in Grimsby, he said, and enfranchisement would only make land dearer and deprive the industrial artisan and others of the humbler classes of those advantages that had been so beneficial to them.[25]

A recurring argument was that leasehold tenure discouraged industry coming to the town.[26] This argument was refuted by John Wintringham in 1888. He argued before a parliamentary committee that leasehold tenure had been to the benefit of Grimsby because it released capital for other investment in the port and enabled building to proceed easily: 'We have developed so fast that I do not think we could have found the money required for buying the freehold.' He considered that freehold tenure would have required an extra quarter of a million pounds of investment in the current housing stock, which was more advantageously employed in other investments in the town: 'in a rapidly expanding town there is not any capital to spare', he said.[27]

None of the local landowners wished to make wholesale changes from the system of 99-year leases but the corporation became engaged in council debates on the rights and wrongs of leasehold tenure. Those supporting leaseholds argued that the ratepayers would lose out if the corporation estate were enfranchised because it would result in a fall in the corporation's income. Also, they said, future generations of ratepayers would be robbed of the benefit of increasing land values. Council member Dr Keetley argued in 1873 that they had valuable property and: 'It was their duty to hand it down, if there was any benefit to arise from it ... As a nobleman's estate descended to his son, so ought the corporation to hand down this property to their successors.'[28]

The volatile nature of the issue is demonstrated in Keetley's about-face 11 years later, when he now supported freehold tenure:

You will find that where land is made freehold there is to be found the greatest improvements and the best buildings; there seems to be a vitality about that class of land – freehold – which is not to be found in leasehold property. Therefore I say to you as a corporation ... assist in benefiting our town as far as possible; because by doing that you will not only benefit trade but you improve the class of building which people erect. You know perfectly well that scarcely any man taking a short lease of say ninety years will build on it a magnificent shop or manufactory.[29]

There were certainly divided opinions on the council, which was partly because some members of the council were corporation lessees. This led to recurring criticisms that councillors' personal interests influenced their attitude to the issue.[30]

Although business lessees may have been dissatisfied with leasehold tenure, it is noticeable that during debates on the question there was no criticism that the houses built on leasehold land were inferior to those built on freehold land. In fact some of the most closely packed or insanitary working-class housing in the town and its neighbourhood was on freehold land. Freehold areas of poor housing included the Clee Allotments, the block of freehold land in Freeman Street and the largely enfranchised plots in the East Marsh Lots and the East Fitty Lots. There is little doubt that, with the exception of some of the housing on the East Marsh, leasehold tenure in general provided a reasonable quality of working-class housing in Grimsby, particularly in comparison with the examples of freehold development.

Clee-with-Weelsby Local Health District

As population and housebuilding on Grant-Thorold and Heneage land in the overspill area increased to meet the needs of Grimsby's persistent industrial growth, there had been increasing concern about the area's public health. Such local government as Clee and Weelsby had was inadequate and was divided between the Caistor poor law union, the Clee parish vestry and the justices of the peace. Consequently, it was suggested in 1875 that the Grimsby boundary should be extended to take in what was a dormitory area. Nothing came of this and in 1877 the area was created a Local Health District and acquired its own local government authority in the form of the Clee-with-Weelsby Local Board of Health. It also got its own School Board and the Hilda Street Board School was built in 1878.[31]

In addition to those already cited, new public buildings in Clee-with-Weelsby included two Primitive Methodist chapels, the Ebenezer (1871) and Hainton Street (1874), St John's Mission Church on Cleethorpe Road (1879) and the Heneage School in Edward Street (1885). By 1880 the area had its own police station in Oxford Street, probably welcomed by members of the Grimsby Christian Vigilante Association who complained of the 'serious harm which the prevalence of brothels within the district is doing'. There were complaints of prostitutes frequenting 'the house of Cawthorne in 5th Terrace, Charles Street'. This street acquired a notorious reputation and following petitions from respectable residents in 1889 it was renamed Hope Street.[32] Under its new optimistic name it achieved a fresh reputation in recent times as Grimsby's best-decorated street on occasions of national and local jubilation.

Financial Postscript

Most of this chapter has been concerned with the effect Heneage had on the locality by developing his land for housing. If we turn the tables and consider the effect of the local housing development on Heneage we find that the ground rents that it produced provided him with a financial lifeline. The 1870s ushered in an agricultural depression that lasted for about thirty years. Consequently, Heneage's income from his vast area of farmland fell from £14,000 in 1870 to £11,000 in 1906. During the same period income from his Grimsby and Weelsby ground rents rose from £3,000 to £8,000 – thus enabling him to keep his head above water during a time of serious farming depression.[33]

Chapter 9

Expansion and Independence
1880s-1891

After its rather shaky start to the century, we have now seen the great surge forward of the town in Victorian times. So much progress had been made that, with assistance from Grant-Thorold and Heneage, it had expanded beyond its boundary, thereby giving birth to the infant Clee-with-Weelsby Local Health District. Had the corporation but known it, this happy event would turn out to be a godsend – as we shall see in this chapter.

The Town in the 1880s

Fortunately, the result of this rapid development was captured by the mapping survey that was carried out during 1886-7 for the first large-scale Ordnance Survey plan of the town. This provides a useful overview of the town in the mid-Victorian period. The plan shows the major changes created in the borough by the MS&LR. The main line sweeps in from Manchester and Sheffield, carving its way through the old town and across the East Marsh to the Royal Dock and Nos 1 and 2 Fish Docks; the dock area bulging out into the Humber on a vast area of reclaimed land. Other MS&LR lines come in from the west serving the Royal Dock and the extended Alexandra Dock. Arrow-straight from the south comes the GNR/ELR line from London, Boston and Louth.

The effect of all this railway and dock activity is shown in the extensive area of mainly working-class housing stretching across the West Marsh and the East Marsh. It then spills over the borough boundary at Humber Street into the Clee Allotments and New Clee. From there it extends as far as the Cleethorpes boundary at Park Street and is just beginning to spread into Cleethorpes. Housing has also spilled over the boundary in the south into Weelsby and has spread down Hainton Avenue as far as Welholme Road. New building extends westerly from the old town, describing a rising curve between the railway line and the River Freshney as far as Haycroft Street. Scattered villa housing is shown along Bargate and in Wellow, where blooms the newly formed People's Park. To the south several hundred acres of farmland lay undeveloped, stretching to the borough boundary, which crosses Scartho Road in the region of the main entrance to the present hospital site.

By this time, the town could boast of three markets: the Old Market, the Central Market and the Freeman Street Market, plus the cattle market in Brighowgate. Goods and passengers were conveyed to and from nearby villages by 50 or so country carriers. Law and order was the concern of the expanding police force with its three police stations at the Town Hall,

57 *Victorian or Edwardian workmen in the Old Market Place.*

Grimsby Coffee Houses

No. 1 House, "THE CENTRAL."
Central Market Place.

Every Accommodation for Visitors, Cyclists, and Commercial Travellers.

First-Class Beds,

SEPARATE ROOMS **1/-** and **1/6** PER NIGHT.

Tea, Coffee and Cocoa, **1d.** per cup, always ready.

DINNERS

EVERY DAY AT TWELVE O'CLOCK.

Roast Beef and Vegetables	...	...	...	**6d.** & **8d.** per plate.
Roast Mutton and Vegetables	...	...	...	**6d.** & **8d.** „
Beef Steak Pudding and Potatoes	...	...	...	**4d.** „
Beef Steak Pie and Potatoes	...	...	...	**4d.** „
Rice Pudding, College Pudding, Jam Roll, or Fruit Tart			...	2d. „

Delicious Chocolate, fresh made, **2d.** per cup.

TEA or COFFEE IN SEPARATE POTS, ONE CUP, **2d.**
TWO CUPS, **3d.**

HAM and EGGS. CHOPS and STEAKS.

HOT WATER FOR TEA.

COMFORT, CLEANLINESS AND MODERATE CHARGES.

No. 2 House—**8 FREEMAN STREET,** Near Cleethorpe Road.
No. 3 House—**29 CLEETHORPE ROAD,** Near Dock Station and Royal Hotel.
No. 4 House—**120 VICTORIA STREET,** Near Town Hall Street.
No. 5 House—**3 CLEETHORPE ROAD, NEW CLEE.**

58 *The Coffee House in the Central Market was in business by 1886. Coffee and Cocoa Houses were frequently set up as teetotal alternatives to public houses.*

Oxford Street and King Edward Street (where the Borough Fire Brigade kept its steam engine). The gas company had started hiring out cookers, fires and bath heaters in 1883; 596 items were hired out in 1887. By the end of the decade, the company had 4,195 consumers and 957 gas lamps lit the town's streets. The post office had a smart new building in West St Mary's Gate, later used as county court offices and even later as a public house/nightclub.

The Theatre Royal in Victoria Street and the Victoria Music Hall in Lower Burgess Street were joined in 1886 by the Prince of Wales Theatre in Freeman Street. Societies and associations included four Masonic lodges, 13 benefit societies and a number of temperance societies. Education was provided by the two Board Schools (Holme Hill and South Parade, plus Hilda Street Board School in Clee-with-Weelsby); other schools included the freemen's schools and several denominational day schools. For the more affluent, the town had a couple of dozen private schools or 'academies', including St James's College (*sic*) on Bargate, which charged 13 guineas per term for boarders plus an extra guinea for 'Washing' – whether for the boys or their clothes was not specified. Other buildings completed during the 1880s included St Paul's Mission Church on Corporation Road (1884), the Dock Offices on Cleethorpe Road (1885), the School of Art in Silver Street (1886), the Victoria Flour Mills in Victoria Street (rebuilt 1889 after a fire in 1888) and the Salvation Army Hall in Duncombe Street (1889) with a smaller hall in Victoria Street. The Scartho Road cemetery was opened in 1889.

Buy-Out Bid

As this diverse community developed in tune with changing needs and expectations, attention was focused on what was regarded as the undue influence that the freeman had in the administration of the borough. Accordingly, non-freeman Councillor King proposed at a council meeting in December 1886 that the Grimsby freemen be approached to see if they would 'entertain in a friendly spirit a proposal to transfer their entire estate, rights and privileges to the Corporation for the benefit of the Ratepayers. Each Freeman and Widow of a Freeman to be compensated by the payment of a lump sum, or such equivalent as may be agreed upon.'[1]

During a long address he mentioned that:

wherever they turned in the work of the Council they came upon the divided authority of the town. None of the gentlemen attending around that table could say that the management of that town was vested in them. The management of the town was carried on by a dual authority – partially by the Corporation and by the Council; and partially by the Pastures Committee, who acted on behalf of the freemen.

He then referred to the divided nature of the local community:

He thought that if they could induce these freemen to throw in their lot with them – to throw the whole into a common fund, and meet upon common grounds as citizens of one community – they would be removing a great deal of jealousy and heart-burning, and doing a good work for the town and the whole community.

He proposed that they should buy from the freemen their holding of £5,800 in consols, their land, their rights of free wharfage, the tolls of the Freeman Street market and the right to free education for freemen's children. He illustrated the decline in the freemen's dividend and how this trend was expected to continue, largely because the number of freemen was increasing. He then suggested offering the freemen £60 each, which, allowing for other costs, came to £50,000. There was general agreement by the council, including freemen members, that his proposal should be put to the Pastures Committee.[2]

The Pastures Committee agreed to get the freemen's response. Its chairman, John Chapman, then had a public letter to his fellow freemen placed in the local press clearly setting out his opinion in favour of selling, both on financial grounds but also because:

> It would extinguish that class feeling which prevails among those who are free and those who are not; it would give to the body corporate of this town the greatest possible freedom of action in all matters where the special interests of the Freemen have to some extent obstructed its mode of procedure, while to the Freemen it would, in my humble opinion, be productive, in the long run, of a permanent good.[3]

A poll of the freemen revealed that most of them were in favour of selling but wanted £80 each. The council offered £70 a head, a total sum of £61,600. After a second poll the number in favour of selling had increased to 624 with 181 against. However, the high hopes on both sides were dashed when the Pastures Committee took legal advice, the crux of which was that the estate was for the benefit of future as well as present freemen. Therefore, the purchase money could not be divided among themselves but would have to be invested and the income from it divided annually. Since the majority of freemen had been attracted to the proposal by the idea of cash in hand, the Pastures Committee immediately decided that it could not recommend the freemen to sell. It informed them that if they had sold their estate and invested the purchase money it would have produced only £1,848 per annum compared with the £3,000 produced by the estate rentals.[4]

The proposal went no further with either the freemen or the corporation. The fact that the borough council were prepared to consider spending such a large amount on the purchase reveals the importance it attached to the transaction. It is significant that both King and Chapman, from different sides, agreed that there were two authorities governing the town.

Public Health and Smallpox

In 1888, Dr D. Page inspected the sanitary condition of Grimsby and Clee-with-Weelsby on behalf of the Local Government Board. He was happy with parts of New Clee, which were 'laid out in streets of good width with four to six-roomed artizans dwellings having commonly ample yard space and not infrequently plots of garden ground at the rear'. However, he criticised other parts, finding fault with insanitary sewers and drains and overfull and leaky wooden box privies that were emptied at intervals of 10 to 14 days.[5] Such criticisms and the outbreak in the locality of a smallpox epidemic during 1887-8 helped to bring to the fore again the idea of the borough extending its boundaries to take in Clee-with-Weelsby. That district needed land for an isolation hospital but Grant-Thorold and Heneage did not want it on their estates because of the effect it could have on land values. So the Grimsby corporation agreed to work with the Clee-with-Weelsby Local Board in the provision of isolation facilities. The Grimsby isolation hospital was on the West Marsh, far from any houses, roughly on the site of the present Joseph Street. A total of 254 patients were admitted to the hospital and 25 persons died in the epidemic.[6]

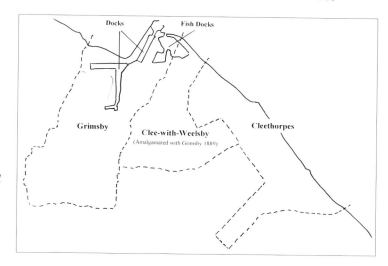

59   *Boundaries between Grimsby, Clee-with-Weelsby and Cleethorpes, 1873-89. In 1889, Clee-with-Weelsby was absorbed into Grimsby and from then on Grimsby's northern boundary with Cleethorpes ran along the middle of Park Street.*

Meanwhile, John Wintringham had become a local hero. By now he was chairman of the Clee-with-Weelsby Local Board and was tireless in organising the hospital provision. He also worked in the isolation hospital himself and visited smallpox victims in their homes. Accordingly, a public subscription was opened for a testimonial to be presented to him in recognition of 'devoted services rendered by him during the late prevalence of smallpox'. He was also rewarded by being made an honorary freeman of Grimsby in January 1889 and made the most of his heroic stature by stating, 'In my opinion it is only by getting rid of the artificial boundary between Grimsby and Clee – a boundary that the smallpox would not respect – and making common ground of both districts ... that we can hope to stamp out the disease'.[7]

Amalgamation and County Borough

If epidemics prepared the ground for amalgamation with Grimsby, the deciding factor was the 1888 Local Government Act, which reorganised local administration across the nation by creating two new local government bodies. These were county councils and county borough councils. The act decreed that existing boroughs with a population of at least 50,000 would become county boroughs and would be effectively self-governing. Smaller boroughs such as Grimsby would lose powers to the new county councils. This hit Grimsby hard because it had been largely self-governing for nearly 700 years but its 1881 population of 28,503 would result in it being subservient to the upstart Lindsey County Council, as would Clee-with-Weelsby. It was thought that rural interests would dominate the county council and consequently Grimsby and neighbourhood would lose out under the new structure.

    Salvation lay in the fact that the populations of both Grimsby and Clee-with-Weelsby had continued to increase rapidly during the 1880s and it was estimated that their joint population by the end of the decade would exceed the requisite fifty thousand. Accordingly, the two authorities put forward a parliamentary bill that would authorise their amalgamation and thus meet the population criteria for county borough status. Grant-Thorold opposed the bill unless his land to the south of Weelsby Road was excluded from the amalgamation; this condition was agreed to by parliament.[8] Strenuous opposition

60 *George Street Methodist Chapel in the early 20th century. It was near the corner directly opposite the present Central Library.*

came from some freemen. Although a majority of the Pastures Committee and freemen agreed to the bill, a vociferous minority campaigned against the proposed extension of their residential area into Clee-with-Weelsby. This was partly to maintain their traditional boundaries but also because a boundary extension would make the estimated 50 freemen who lived in Clee-with-Weelsby eligible to receive the annual dividend, thereby reducing the amount received by each freeman. This objection was rejected by parliament, with the result that henceforth freemen who chose to reside in any part of the enlarged borough would be eligible to share in the annual dividend. The act came into effect on 1 October 1889, creating a borough with a population of 51,934 in 1891. Application was then made for the greatly enlarged municipal borough to become a county borough. This was agreed and the independent Grimsby County Borough came into existence on 1 April 1891. A day of celebration was held in People's Park on 9 April, which included a musical programme by two bands, a horse show and a 'Grand Fireworks Display'.[9]

Such was the relief of the corporation on the achievement of county borough status that it granted the honorary freedom of the borough to several people to whom it felt gratitude for the advancement of the town. One was Sir Edward Watkin, whose honorary freedom we have already mentioned, and another was Edward Heneage. As one of the two major landowners in the area to be absorbed into Grimsby, Heneage's strong support of the extension bill had been essential, particularly in view of Grant-Thorold's initial opposition. And as the borough's Member of Parliament he then used his parliamentary influence to get the bill successfully enacted. Even though he had been elected an alderman in the new Lindsey County Council he had campaigned there for Grimsby to have county borough status. After the county council had agreed to this, he then got parliamentary approval for Grimsby to be a county borough with its own quarter sessions. He also argued successfully that the town and nearby parishes should constitute a new Grimsby poor law union. Since 1836 what was now the largest town in Lincolnshire had been part of the Caistor union. When the freedom was conferred on Heneage in April 1891 the mayor of Grimsby said that it was 'largely due to his efforts that they were there that evening to celebrate Grimsby becoming a county borough'.[10]

61 *St Mary's Roman Catholic Church at Holme Hill, showing part of the highly decorated interior. The wall decoration was later painted over but it is currently being uncovered (in stages) and restored to its original splendour.*

62 *Most denominations established mission churches in areas of new building. This is the King Terrace Methodist Mission at its closure in 1961. King Terrace was part of the close-packed housing to the west of Doughty Road and south of the railway line.*

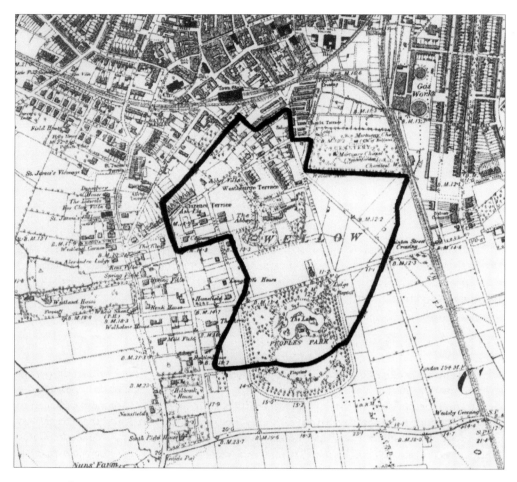

63 *Wellow (within the bold line) in 1887. Years of dispute over to what extent it was part of Grimsby came to an end with the boundary extension of 1889 when it became definitely part of the borough.*

Wellow

One effect of the 1889 extension act was to clear up a quandary regarding Wellow, which was land in the Heneage estate that lay in the People's Park area. In medieval times Wellow was under the jurisdiction of Wellow Abbey and uncertainty regarding to what extent it was part of Grimsby continued into the 19th century. From 1851 Wellow had contributed to Grimsby's general municipal rate and the census report for 1871 confidently stated that 'this hamlet is now considered to be within the Municipal Borough'. However, the town clerk, William Grange, said that it was not in the borough even though its residents paid rates to Grimsby and voted in Grimsby's municipal elections. The matter became controversial in 1878 as a result of Heneage's building operations in Wellow. Consequently, a legal opinion was obtained (probably requested by Heneage's agent, John Wintringham) that concluded that the 'Hamlet of Wellow' was not part of the borough. If this opinion had been allowed to stand after the 1889 boundary extension, Wellow would have been an independent enclave surrounded by land of the enlarged borough. Accordingly, the 1889 act decreed that the 'Hamlet of Wellow' was indeed part of the borough of Grimsby.

Chapter 10

Controversial Times

1890s

The boundary extension and achievement of county borough status in 1891 was a high point in the town's development, emphasising its advancement, enterprise and importance both within the county and the country. But problems lay ahead for the fledgling county borough.

West Marsh Mixed Fortunes

After the euphoria of gaining county borough status had died away there followed a period of mixed fortunes for the corporation's estate policy. It had been very successful in leasing the West Marsh for building in the 1870s and 1880s but a change in corporation policy then left sizeable areas of land undeveloped. This arose because of the likelihood that the railway company would construct a new dock on the foreshore to the north of the Alexandra Dock. As the council discussed leasing land on the West Marsh in 1895, it was remarked that the land would not realise its full value if leased at present because of the possibility of 'great improvements' by the railway company.[1] The corporation's expectations of the rising land values led it to hold land vacant during the 1890s and into the new century.

Other landowners were quite happy to take advantage of the corporation's halt in granting leases. Frederick Tennyson was still leasing out land in the old town and had 20 houses built in West Dock Street during the 1890s. Then, in the 1890s and early 1900s, he had about 80 houses built on his land along the west side of Alexandra Road in the West Marsh. His adjoining land was built up as Frederick Street, Alfred Street, Davison Avenue and Somersby Street, while he had more houses built in Fildes Street and South Parade.

Alderman (later Sir) George Doughty (1854-1914) was also happy to build on the marsh. Doughty was a local man who made a fortune in housebuilding and then invested in the fishing industry. A long-time member of the town council, then town mayor and Grimsby's Member of Parliament, he was knighted in 1904. He had previously purchased a strip of land alongside the dock estate and built this up to create the eastern side of Alexandra Road. During the period 1895-1906, more than 260 leasehold terraced houses were built on Tennyson and Doughty land in the Alexandra Road area.[2] Builders continued to apply for corporation land elsewhere on the West Marsh but to no avail.

In the meantime, the question of using corporation land for public recreation was raised again in 1893 and 1894 when the idea was revived of a 'boulevard' along the side of the River Freshney in order to mark the marriage of the Duke of York. Accordingly, about eight acres were used to create the Duke of York Gardens and Pleasure Grounds, which were opened in 1894. It is an indication of the corporation's ambivalence over the issue that not enough thought or finance was given to their maintenance and in 1904 comment was made of the neglected recreation grounds on the West Marsh and the rubbish in the adjacent River Freshney.[3]

East End Closes

The only other sizeable area of corporation land was the East End Closes, which were largely taken up with public-related buildings such as the Town Hall, freemen's schools, cemetery and gasworks. Railway lines also divided it, so only about eight acres had any potential for house building. The corporation decided to use part of the land for a major public road, Doughty Road, which would pass under the railway lines. Completed in 1895, this was a badly needed public facility and replaced the Peppercorn Walk pedestrian level crossing. It also gave improved access to the remaining corporation land. Just over half an acre of this was used for the only housing there, almshouses erected by public subscription in 1897 to mark Queen Victoria's Diamond Jubilee. The remaining vacant land was used for the corporation-owned electricity works, highways yard, stables, refuse destructor and factory and workshop buildings.[4]

64   *Development on the corporation's East End Closes – Doughty Road underpass and the cooling towers of the corporation electricity works.*

Public Nuisances and Pollution

The 1890s saw no major improvement in the corporation's lax attitude towards the control of building and public health. An instance of the town's public health problems arose on the West Marsh. Although the primary and most likely use of the West Marsh was seen to be for housing, one of the reasons given for bridging the old dock had been to make the land available for 'trade premises'.[5] By selling land to the MS&LR for the Alexandra Dock extension, the corporation accepted that industry would be sited in close proximity to housing. Indeed, the Alexandra Dock, timber yards and a railway line along the route of what is now Boulevard Avenue soon hemmed in the estate. Therefore, the West Marsh was inevitably going to be seen as a source of land for both working-class housing and industry.

It is not surprising that this mixture resulted in complaints of public nuisances. Sawmill chimneys produced pollution and led to complaints of breaches of leasehold covenants. A greater nuisance was the corporation's own night soil depot in the extreme north-western corner of the West Marsh. The corporation later moved it a short distance into Little Coates. But it attracted complaints from Peter Dixon's nearby paper mill that flies from it were getting on to calendar rollers and spoiling white paper.[6]

65 *Postcard 'Grimsby's Scent Bottle', postmarked 1907. It refers to the West Marsh 'stink' from fishmeal works. On the reverse is written 'Hope you like this postcard. It is the latest. We're going to sell this at 4/- a bottle.'*

The most persistent complaints were of smells from fishmeal fertiliser factories. Even before leasing began, a fishmeal works was located on the West Marsh. It was owned by a member of the corporation and was criticised for causing a public nuisance. In May 1873 the MS&LR directors were advised that 'great complaints' had been made by the company's tenants of a nuisance caused by the 'Bone and Manure Works' in the West Marsh. It was decided to ask Dr Letherby, Professor of Chemistry and Medical Officer of Health for the City of London, to visit the works and report thereon. Letherby visited Grimsby on 21 May and reported that he:

noticed a very offensive smell of decomposing animal matters. In the open yard of the premises there was a large accumulation of putrid flesh and bones in a most disgusting condition and within the Works were many scores of loads of the refuse of Cooked Fishes Livers and of the Bones of Haddocks Heads – all of which were undergoing the usual putrefactive decomposition and were evolving a nauseous sickening odour.[7]

Two railway wagons full of fish heads entered the premises at the time of his visit and he commented that the operations were 'conducted in a most slovenly manner, without any regard for public comfort'. He said the matter required immediate attention and that the corporation already had the necessary powers to start the legal process for removing the nuisance. The only effect was that the works was later transferred a short distance beyond the borough boundary into Little Coates. The problems with fishmeal works continued over the decades and one issue of a newspaper in 1905 carried five letters regarding the smell. One of the letters complained that:

> The stench made me sick. It was quite as horrible as anything we have had in the history of this scandalous nuisance ... How the people in the Town Council have the effrontery to defend it I really do not know. The fact is they love dividends better than their fellows. Let the people in the Marsh and neighbourhood rise in a body against the outrage. [signed] One of the Victims.[8]

There is a clear accusation here that members of the borough council had commercial interests in the factories and were letting this influence their approach to the problem. Eventually, the corporation prosecuted the Grimsby Fish and Oil Manure Company whose factory was in Little Coates. The company was found guilty of causing a nuisance by offensive smells and was fined £5 with £3 18s. 2d. costs. Three weeks after this ineffective 'punishment' the stench was as bad as ever and residents complained that, 'We people who live in the West Marsh are being simply poisoned by smells from the manure works.' This particular company later moved its factory some miles away.[9]

Running the Town

During the 1890s, several events occurred which highlighted influences that were brought to bear on the borough council as it strived to administer the town. One of these was the influence of landed magnates, such as that which we have seen exerted by Lord Yarborough and George Heneage during the 1850s public health controversy. Edward Heneage highlighted such influence when he appeared before a parliamentary committee on railway bills in 1891. Asked about his interest in the town, he replied:

> For the last 25 years I have been intimately connected and in full touch with every interest of the port and town. I do not think there is either a single improvement or a single question of anything to develop in the town and trade of Grimsby which I have not had a hand in or been consulted upon.[10]

He justified this by saying that, 'My family have been there for 300 years, and my father was a director of the East Lincolnshire line which has now been absorbed in the Great Northern, and was also largely instrumental in the development of the Manchester and Sheffield [MS&LR] Docks and the [railway] extension to Grimsby.'

Heneage vs. Grant-Thorold

This attitude of mind came to public attention in the 1890s in respect of building on the Heneage and Grant-Thorold estates. While leasing had stopped or slowed on the estates of the corporation and the freemen, there was no slow down on the Heneage estate in Weelsby and Wellow. To the east of the GNR/ELR line (now used for the Peaks Parkway) building continued down Hainton Avenue, Heneage Road, Convamore Road and side streets. To the west of the railway line, building had taken place on Wintringham Road, Patrick Street, Welholme Road, Legsby Avenue and Farebrother Street. Further west, in Wellow, housing now occupied land to the north of People's Park. Infilling with villas had taken place along Welholme Avenue and the eastern side of Bargate. However, despite the attractive location, only about five villas had been built on the land surrounding People's Park. There was no lack of demand from builders but Heneage would not permit speculative building around the park. This policy was designed to create an exclusive area of owner-occupied high-quality villas.

One reason why Heneage was able to extend his building to such a great extent lay in his machinations regarding the adjacent Grant-Thorold estate. A sizeable area of the latter's estate was turned over to building but much more would have been built-up if Heneage had been co-operative. It may seem odd that, despite all the fulsome praise that Heneage received in 1891 when he was granted the freedom of the borough, he was defeated at the general election a year later. Putting honorary freedoms and politics to one side, he was being heavily criticised for holding back further town development. The matter first arose in 1877 when Grant-Thorold wanted to open up for building a large area of his land south of Oxford Street. To do this he needed road access into Wellington Street, which would then give him access into Freeman Street and the docks. To get this access he had to cross Heneage land, but Heneage refused his request in order to keep his own land at a premium for building.[11] Another request was turned down in 1883.

However, Heneage had a block of over 100 acres of land by Clee village (known nowadays as Old Clee), which lay the other side of Grant-Thorold's land. Consequently, when Grant-Thorold renewed his request in 1887 Heneage agreed, subject to two conditions. The first was that in return he be granted road access over Grant-Thorold land to Clee village, which would have increased the value of his land there. The second was that Grant-Thorold should give 20 acres of land as a children's playground on his heavily built-up estate.[12] Grant-Thorold did not accede to these terms, presumably not being overjoyed at the thought of 20 acres of his valuable building land being used for a playground.

For the next five years the issue lay unresolved as Heneage happily continued his extensive building development. After 1891 the new county borough council began to put pressure on the two bickering landowners to resolve their differences for the benefit of the town. In April 1892 it expressed concern at the 'blocks' that Heneage had erected at the end of some of his streets where they met Grant-Thorold's land. Heneage's response in June 1892 illustrated once more the attitude of local landed magnates to the wishes of the elected authority. He stated that he was 'not prepared to bow to the dictation of the Town Council in their intervention between one landlord and another.'[13] Despite this rebuff, one month later the corporation was considering a report and plan by borough surveyor John Buchan for a comprehensive new road layout that would extend several of Heneage's roads across Grant-Thorold land to Cleethorpes. The report made the point that:

> The time has now arrived when some definite ... scheme should be agreed upon between the corporation and the landowners for dealing with the entire district and its future main arteries of traffic ... no such scheme as this exists, each landowner laying out his land to the best commercial advantage from his own point of view.[14]

Under Buchan's plan, Wellington Street, Pasture Street, Eleanor Street and Welholme Road would all have been extended from the Heneage estate boundary across Grant-Thorold land, the latter two providing main roads through to Cleethorpes. Heneage's devious response was to agree publicly to the proposals but to write privately to Wintringham on 13 August 1892 that:

> Whilst I have given consent to the Town Council Schemes, there is no reason why we should hurry about it; and I think with judicious management and the alterations sure to be suggested ... we might calculate upon it not arriving at even an agreement for another six months and the roads will take quite a year before they are completed ... so that we might get a good deal of land leased ... I feel certain that Mr Thorold will not make the Welholme Road extension and would be a fool if he did.[15]

Nothing came of the scheme and when Grant-Thorold submitted plans in 1893 for future building on his land the Borough Surveyor commented that while his land could accommodate a population of 70,000 there was no provision 'for an open square or site for Public Recreation or breathing space whatever'.[16]

There was little sign of movement until 1895. Heneage had regained his parliamentary seat at a by-election but there was an impending general election and he was coming in for increasing criticism for holding up town development for his own gain. Wintringham advised Heneage that he would like to get the 'blocks' down as early as possible as he did not want them to be used as 'an election cry against you'. However, he could not advise removing the blocks at the ends of Wellington Street and Eleanor Street until they had road access to the land at Clee, which would mean 'thousands of pounds difference to your estate'. The matter was not resolved before the election in July, which Heneage lost by 181 votes but was compensated with a peerage the following year.[17]

It was not until 1897, 20 years after the dispute had begun, that Wintringham advised Heneage to take down the Wellington Street block because he had been assured of road access to the Clee land. He wrote that the block 'will have served you well ... having enabled you to lease your Building Land much further up than you could otherwise have done'. Even so, another year passed before Heneage said with little grace that 'Mr Thorold can take down the block at his convenience; the bricks will pay for the labour.'[18] That building soon began in this area of Grant-Thorold land is shown by the street names reflecting the Boer War of 1899-1902, such as Ladysmith Road, Roberts Street and Buller Street. Grant-Thorold gave nine acres (not the 20 acres stipulated by Heneage) for an open space, on the self-congratulatory condition that it was called the Grant-Thorold Park. It was opened on 30 June 1904 to the accompaniment of cowboy gunfire and Red Indian war cries from the touring Buffalo Bill Wild West Show, which was being held in a nearby field. As a postscript, it is ironic that only a small proportion of Heneage's land near Clee village has been used for housing. At the time of writing most of it is used for allotments and school playing fields.

The Enrolled Freemen

Other disputes were between the corporation and the freemen. Because of the retention of some of their ancient rights and privileges the freemen were able to affect the corporation's administration. We have seen that questions began to be asked about who was running the town, the elected corporation or the unrepresentative freemen. The main thrust of late 19th-century complaints was that the freemen were a privileged minority who profited on the back of the efforts of the rest of the town. They were also thought to wield power at the expense of the remainder of the population and act generally to the detriment of the borough. This led to a comment in 1871 that, 'There is a growing feeling in the country that such feudal monopolies should be extinguished.'[19]

There was also criticism that the freemen's interests were too well represented on the borough council, which gave them extra influence. A niggling dispute during the 1880s was to what extent the freemen should benefit from the sale of a dockside wharf that the corporation owned but in which the freemen had the right of free use, leading Councillor Alward to remark that he:

> was very sorry that there was such a sect as the freemen of the borough. It was a pity that land, virtually belonging to the burgesses [ratepayers] of the borough, should be claimed by other people, and he hoped to see the day come when there would be no such thing as dividing land.[20]

Another cause for complaint was the fact that the freemen opposed new developments that were of importance to the whole town. Examples were their opposition to the corporation's 1869 Improvement Act and its 1889 Extension Act, which we have noted above.

William Grange

The strained relations between the town and the freemen were not eased by William Grange's dual role of town clerk and clerk to the freemen. Even his solicitor partner, John Wintringham, remarked, 'I have sometimes thought that my partner was too much of a freeman – that he was too anxious for the rights and privileges of his order.'[21] Grange appeared to agree with this when he was presented with the honorary freedom of the borough in 1899 and in his acceptance speech made a public declaration of his loyalty to the enrolled freemen's interests:

> I am one of the freemen of the old stock. I assisted the freemen fifty years ago to obtain their act of parliament and since then in improving and developing their valuable estates. There is no other body of freemen in the kingdom so highly favoured as are the freemen of Grimsby ... I am second to none in loyalty to their interests.[22]

The difficulty of his position in holding both posts was commented on in a local newspaper, to the effect that, although he acted fairly, 'the position has to be faced; the freemen's interests, broadly speaking, are not those of the Commonality of the Borough, and the town clerk is, willy-nilly, the legal adviser of both'.[23]

The Freemen's Schools

One dispute concerned the freemen's schools. By the 1860s the schools were housed in two purpose-built buildings, one for boys and one for girls. These still stand, with other uses, either side of the Town Hall. They were built on corporation land and financed by the corporation. As the number of freemen's children increased, the schools became inadequate. There then followed from the 1870s a long-running controversy. The freemen complained of insufficient places at the schools for their children while non-freemen complained of the cost of the schools to the ratepayers.[24]

In 1903 the corporation became the local education authority under the 1902 Education Act and decided that the schools should be thrown open to the public. In response the freemen decided that, if necessary, they would take legal action to protect their rights in the schools and the matter was left in abeyance.[25] In 1905 the corporation proposed that the schools should be closed and offered 75 scholarships for freemen's children at the Grimsby Municipal College. The freemen's response was unyielding, again threatening legal action. Another attempt to resolve the issue was made in 1921 but it was not until 1949 that the corporation obtained parliamentary approval to close what were then referred to as the 'inconvenient and unsatisfactory schools'.[26]

The Freeman Street Market

The issue of the Freeman Street Market was even more contentious. When the freemen laid out the East Marsh for building in 1859, an area was set aside for a market on Freeman Street but no attempt was made to establish one. By the 1870s a market was being called for by residents and the Pastures Committee saw a way of achieving this at no cost to the freemen. There had been a long-standing dispute between the corporation and the freemen about an acre of unused land on the East Marsh Fitties to which both laid claim. The Pastures Committee proposed that the corporation should sell the disputed land and use the proceeds to finance the construction of a market square on the Freeman Street plot. In return, the freemen offered to give up to the corporation all their rights and interests in the market plot. The borough council accepted the proposal. It would be a face-saving end to the dispute and the corporation would acquire the ownership of a market and market square. From the freemen's point of view, their estate and land values would be improved by the provision of an important public facility at no cost to themselves. The sale of the disputed land raised £862, which paid for the market square to be laid out, and the Freeman Street Market opened on 2 September 1873.[27]

The corporation now believed that it owned the market square and the market. However, its legal advisor and town clerk, William Grange, should have prevented them from walking into a legal minefield. Under the terms of the Pastures Act, the freemen could only dispose of their land by public auction. Therefore, the freemen could argue that the corporation's presumed ownership of the market square was invalid. The corporation officers and members compounded the situation by failing to set up a proper system of control. As a result, while the corporation paid for the upkeep of the market, the Pastures Committee was allowed to collect and keep some of the market rents. Members of the borough council complained that the freemen were taking rents from the market while the cost of upkeep was being borne by the ratepayers. They went on to say that 'this created a soreness in the minds of non-freemen' and the doubt should be cleared up as to whether the market was the property of the corporation or the freemen. Grange, in his role as clerk to the freemen, said that the freemen had the power to take possession of the market place altogether if they wanted to.[28]

Discussion and confrontation over the years failed to settle the matter and, on 8 May 1903, a leader in the *Grimsby News* commented that it seemed incredible that

66 *The freemen's Girls' School, built 1863. Later it housed the Doughty Museum in 1958 and then the Doughty Centre. It is seen here in 1989. The freemen's Boys' School on the other side of the Town Hall (now the register office) was built in 1867.*

67 *Freeman Street Market in the early 1900s, when the corporation and the freemen were disputing its ownership. The market opened in 1873 and became a covered market in 1959.*

68 *Victoria Street and horse-drawn tram, 1890s. West St Mary's Gate leads off on the extreme right.*

the corporation did not know whether the market square belonged to 'the town' or the freemen:

> some useful work might be done if ... the general relations of the freemen and the corporation could be gone into, for there seems to be no definite line to show where the rights and interests of the freemen end and those of the corporation begin. We put the matter in this way because it does seem that all the privilege is on the side of the freemen. We suppose the freemen's rights and privileges come to them ... simply through the accident of birth, and it certainly appears that ... [they] have not been slow to increase and care for their material interest.[29]

In response, a resolution was passed at the freemen's annual meeting a month later that if necessary they would, 'defend proceedings in the Court of Chancery for the protection of the Freemen's rights and interests in the Grammar Schools, Freeman Street Market Square, and the Freemen's estates in general'.[30]

Such was the level of discord between the town and the freemen that the *Grimsby News* ran a series of 12 articles on the history and current ramifications of the freemen and their rights and privileges. The series ran during July-September 1903, was written anonymously by an 'Ex-Representative Freeman' and was critical of the freemen's claims. It compared the corporation and the freemen as, 'The one with many duties and few privileges and the other with many privileges and few or no obligations.' It declared that '65,000 inhabitants are at a disadvantage as compared with the freemen ... [who] monopolise estates which belonged to the municipality as a whole'.[31]

There followed a period of intense belligerence on the part of the freemen with regard to the market and schools question, some of their language being redolent of that used by the freemen of the 1840s. As an example, the annual meeting in 1904 was chaired by watchmaker and jeweller Joseph Ward who was asked whether he would agree to the corporation 'robbing' (*sic*) the freemen of the market. He replied with an emphatic, 'No ... if the Corporation wanted the market they would fight. The freemen would not part with it ... During the year the rents had realised something like £400 ... If they should ask for it they would find, like the Russians, they had something to meet. (Hear, Hear).'[32]

The *Grimsby News* commented on the bellicose attitude:

> How valiant the freemen are. They are prepared to fight the corporation over the Freeman Street Market. Some of the rank and file seem to have got it into their heads that the corporation is trying to 'rob' them of the marketplace ... A nice amiable sort of attitude showing a tender regard for the welfare of the community at large.[33]

69   *Prince of Wales Theatre in Freeman Street, decorated in 1897 during the jubilee celebrations that marked Queen Victoria's 60 years on the throne.*

70 *Grimsby in 1887, showing the built-up East Marsh and the partly developed West Marsh. On the right, housing had spilled over into Clee (as far as the Cleethorpes boundary at Park Street). Weelsby to the south was being built up and People's Park lay in the largely unbuilt Wellow.*

71 *Grimsby, 1905. By now building had spilled into Cleethorpes, creating the dormitory suburb of New Cleethorpes along Grimsby Road. To the south, extensive building in Weelsby had nearly reached Weelsby Road.*

Despite calls at council meetings for a Local Government Board inquiry into the market question, no progress was made and both the freemen and the town clerk were criticised in council with regard to the 'unjust treatment of this Council by the Freemen and their legal advisor' (i.e. William Grange). Later in the same year, 1904, the corporation acknowledged defeat and accepted the freemen's ownership and control of the market.[34]

New Cleethorpes

In addition to its strained relations with local landowners and the freemen, the corporation was on uneasy terms with neighbouring Cleethorpes. The housing that had spilled over the Grimsby boundary into Cleethorpes at Park Street now formed a large area of better quality, mainly working-class housing. It had become known as New Cleethorpes and was separated from the resort area of Cleethorpes by green fields. It was effectively a dormitory suburb of Grimsby because its residents worked overwhelmingly in the Grimsby dock industries. It would be an attractive financial prize if the port could acquire it, bringing with it a sizeable annual income in municipal rates, which would be a welcome addition to the borough's coffers. Accordingly, in 1893 the Grimsby borough council proposed obtaining parliamentary permission to take in New Cleethorpes by extending the borough boundary to the foot of Isaacs Hill. The proposal was withdrawn in the face of uncompromising opposition 'to the bitter end' from Cleethorpes.[35] Mainly in an attempt to forestall any further moves by Grimsby, Cleethorpes Urban District Council tried to gain more power by applying to the Privy Council in 1897 for a grant of borough status. Grimsby council objected to the grant and the Cleethorpes application failed, which did not improve the relationship between the two authorities.[36]

New Buildings and Services

Grimsby's population continued to increase during the 1890s and new churches and chapels included All Saints' (corrugated iron) Church in Heneage Road (1891), the Church of St John the Divine in Albion Street (1891-2), the Arlington Street Wesleyan Church (1892), Hilda Street Wesleyan Chapel (1892), the Congregational Mission Church in Granville Street (1895) and the Welholme Road Primitive Methodist Chapel (1897). The port missioner held daily services in the Sailors' and Fishermen's Harbour of Refuge in Thesiger Street. New schools included the James Meadows School in Weelsby Street (1890), the Welholme Road School East (1892) and the Wintringham Higher Grade School in Eleanor Street (1895, and destined to have several guises, eventually becoming the Wintringham Grammar School). By the end of the century, the town had over 40 places of worship and about 25 Board, denominational or charity schools, including a Ragged School in Albert Street.

Other developments included a new drainage works and pumping station (1895), the consecration of the Jewish cemetery (1896), the opening of the Artillery Volunteer Barracks in Victoria Street North (1891, later becoming Albert Gait's printing works) and the opening of the Scartho Road workhouse (1894). A sign of technical change was the coming of electrical power; in 1891 electric lamps were installed in the Town Hall. 1894 saw the corporation obtaining powers to supply electricity and in 1899 the foundation stone of the corporation's Moss Road electricity generating station was laid.

Chapter 11

Star of the East Coast?

1900-1914

Writing in 1913, our old friend, freeman and Grimsby patriot Bob Lincoln had hope and belief that his native town would become a great industrial centre and the 'Star of the East Coast'.[1] His belief was inspired by the town's achievements during the past century, but the attainment of star status would depend to a large extent on what was happening 'down dock'.

Running Out of Dock Space

As the town entered the new century, fishing was still king. The busy Easter Week landings in 1902 totalled 4,641 tons, leading to the comment, 'It might be interesting to note that if the 1,547 wagons employed in the despatch of fish during Easter Week 1902, were placed end to end, they would extend for 5 miles or over.' In 1907, 160,392 tons were forwarded over the kingdom, rising to 193,363 tons in 1912. By 1912 the port's registered fleet consisted of 587 steam fishing boats and 23 sailing vessels and was also used extensively by fishing boats registered elsewhere. This level of activity was being carried out in what had become woefully inadequate fish docks. After strong local representations the GCR belatedly obtained the Great Central Railway (Grimsby Fish Docks) Act in 1912, which authorised the construction of a new dock adjoining the existing fish docks. The outbreak of the First World War brought any construction plans to a halt.[2]

The commercial docks were also proving to be inadequate for the level of trade. Between 1898 and 1911, the value of imports rose from £7.75 million to £13.5 million and the value of exports rose from £11 million to £20 million. Coal and timber figured large, over 1.6 million tons of coal being exported in 1911 and timber imports running at over 300,000 tons annually. Other trade included textile fabrics and manufactures, iron and steel manufactures, machinery, dairy products, bacon, grains and metal ores. Steamers made regular sailings to Hamburg, Rotterdam, Antwerp, Dieppe, Malmo, Helsingborg, Gothenburg and Esbjerg, plus frequent boats to London, Hull and other home ports. As with the fish trade, more dock accommodation was needed. A new commercial dock north of the Alexandra Dock was proposed but the GCR maintained that it would need a local subsidy if its construction were to be financially viable. Accordingly, in 1900, 13 local landowners, banks and businesses agreed to make a combined contribution of £5,000 per annum for seven years, of which the corporation agreed to contribute £500 per annum.[3] This bounteous offer of financial support came to nothing because in 1904 the projected location was moved to Immingham to take advantage of the deep-water channel.

72 *The Carisbrooke, representative of the many and varied steam trawlers that superseded the sailing smacks and fished from Grimsby in the 20th century.*

73 *Grimsby trawler crew and part of their catch.*

Immingham and the Clickety

The decision to construct a dock at Immingham was a blow to the town. The corporation argued that the dock should be incorporated into the borough. The corporation's supporters included Heneage, who envisaged that Grimsby would annex Immingham and the intervening land and create a 'Liverpool of the East' along the Humber bank. Despite Heneage's support, the bid failed because of uncompromising opposition from the Lindsey County Council. The county council was not prepared to 'allow a big slice of rateable territory to be absorbed by Grimsby without a struggle'.[4] Dock construction began at Immingham in 1906 and it was anticipated that the completed dock would draw most of its labour from Grimsby. Accordingly, the GCR was granted a light-railway order for an electric tramway to be constructed from a junction with the tram lines in Victoria Street. From there it would run over the Corporation Bridge and on to the Immingham dock estate. Initially, there was just a temporary line for construction workmen. It operated for about four years between Immingham and the vicinity of the present Boulevard Avenue. In 1910 the service was opened to the public. In 1912 it began operating from a terminus near the Corporation Bridge and became known as the 'Clickety' from the sound of its wheels on the track.[5] The plan to cross the Corporation Bridge was never implemented and the 'Clickety' was closed down on 1 July 1961. George V and Queen Mary opened the Immingham Dock in 1912.

Little Coates

In the meantime, the corporation had been waiting for the good times to start rolling regarding its remaining West Marsh land, but once again another landowner started building while

74   *Henderson Jetty at Grimsby when fish was king.*

75   *Riverhead c.1900. The steam vessel on the left is believed to be unloading sacks of flour from Hull while the barge is said to be unloading bags of cement from Melton on the north bank of the Humber.*

the corporation dithered. In 1898, Sir Walter Gilbey had purchased most of the parish of Little Coates, part of which ran alongside the West Marsh. His land was physically cut off from the marsh by the GCR Great Coates branch line that ran to the docks. In 1901 the GCR agreed to move the line to the other side of Little Coates. This gave the impetus to the opening up of Gilbey's land for development, which began to take off when Peter Dixon & Son of Oughtibridge, Sheffield, constructed a paper mill in Little Coates just outside the Grimsby boundary. The site was chosen because it had good port facilities nearby and access to a good supply of fresh water. The mill opened in 1906 and a local newspaper reported that 'two new streets of houses have sprung up suggesting a new colony'. In its early days the mill had over 200 workers and by 1912 had grown to become the largest in Europe (it was closed down in 1973).[6] Gilbey's land was rapidly developed, producing the housing that lies either side of Gilbey Road, between Elsenham Road and the River Freshney. The re-located Great Coates branch line reopened in 1909. Its old track became Boulevard Avenue.

The Cow Close

In 1908 the Little Coates house building finally spurred on the corporation to release its vacant land on the West Marsh. This included part of the Cow Close, which was land between the River Freshney and Macaulay Street. The corporation's portion of the Cow Close was leased for the construction of small working-class houses, which were still in short supply. The freemen continued to have difficulty attracting builders to the Little Field and the Haycroft. Their only new building up to the end of the previous century was along Cromwell Road and the Pastures Committee was criticised in 1904 because it had allowed good-quality houses in Cromwell Road to be turned into shops:

The effect of which has been to drive several people from the neighbourhood and cause houses to be hard to let ... It is a pity that one of the finest streets in the whole town – that is what people say who are in the habit of using Cromwell Road – should be spoiled by this small-shop business. The Freemen already begin to see a mistake has been made.[7]

There was persistent pressure on the Pastures Committee to increase the estate income as the number of freemen grew and their dividend declined. The Haycroft included part of the Cow Close, which by now contained the corporation development of small houses. Therefore, in November 1913, at what was to be its last major leasing of land before the outbreak of the First World War, the Pastures Committee put up for auction nearly four acres of building land in the Cow Close. About three and a half acres were taken, which were planned to accommodate 150 mainly small working-class houses on plots of approximately 100 square yards. The auction produced a welcome addition of £100 to the annual rent roll.[8] The building abutted the existing corporation housing and the joint Cow Close development lay either side of Lord Street, between Boulevard Avenue and Haycroft Avenue. It included those streets that may be identified by the use of Christian names such as Joseph Street, James Street, Richard Street, etc.

At the outbreak of war in 1914, 25 acres in the Little Field and the Haycroft were still in agricultural use. The freemen had been successful since 1859 in leasing or selling most of their estate and in 1914 had approximately eight hundred leasehold tenants, plus 89 tenants of paddocks and gardens. Of their rental of £3,202 in 1914, 95 per cent came from building leases.[9]

Building on the Heneage and Grant-Thorold Estates

Building was flourishing on the Heneage and Grant-Thorold estates. Grant-Thorold had sold the Weelsby Old Hall part of his estate to local brewer William Taylor Hewitt in 1890, moved to London and died there in 1908. Building continued on the remainder of the estate and also on the Heneage estate as housing spread southwards. Heneage in particular was doing well. By 1905 Hainton Avenue and Heneage Road were built up as far as Algernon Street. Land between Algernon Street and Weelsby Road was sold by Heneage to trawler magnate Sir George Sleight and features roads named after his company's trawlers – Reporto Avenue, Responso Avenue and so on. Heneage land in and around Wellow was extensively developed, including more building in Farebrother Street, Legsby Avenue and the area between Wintringham Road and Welholme Road. Work on the 'Avenues' area off Weelsby Road began and the early months of 1914 saw plans approved for the construction of Eastwood Avenue and Portland Avenue. Improvements proposed for Weelsby Road included a 60-feet wide subway under the GNR line and the widening of the road to 72 feet between the subway and Nuns Corner.[10]

Public Transport, Suburbs and Commuter Villages

In addition to the building in Little Coates, overspill led to the further growth of New Cleethorpes. There was also increasing residential development in the vicinity of the railway halts at such places as North Thoresby, Great Coates, Healing and New Waltham. The latter halt was near to Humberston Avenue and in 1901 the owner of Humberston,

76   *The busy Old Market Place and the Corn Exchange in 1910.*

Lord Carrington, put up for sale land in the avenue that he intended to set out with new roads and house plots, but as late as 1920 only a few villas had been built there.

Cleethorpes commuters had for long been making use of the train service to Grimsby while the tram system assisted development by making it more convenient for the workforce to live in the newly developing parts of the borough and Cleethorpes. The conversion of the trams to electricity on 7 December 1901 saw increased use. In their last full year of working, the horse trams carried just over two million passengers; this jumped to six million in the first full year of electric working. Fares were cheap: 1d. for any journey in Grimsby and 2d. from Grimsby to the Cleethorpes terminus. Motorbuses began to appear on the scene and the tram company started bus services to Waltham and Caistor in 1909 and 1910.[11]

Another Bid for Boundary Extensions

The corporation had not given up hope of incorporating the new Immingham Dock into the borough and tried again in 1907. On this occasion it was part of a wide-ranging proposal to extend the borough boundary. This would take in Immingham Dock, the dormitory suburb of New Cleethorpes, part of Great Coates, the built-up portion of Little Coates (Gilbey Road etc.) and the extensive undeveloped area of Weelsby south of Weelsby Road (now including the Weelsby Woods park). The Lindsey County Council was still stubbornly against the idea of losing the valuable Immingham Dock and other rateable land. Other determined opponents to parts of the proposal included the Cleethorpes Urban District Council and the Grimsby Rural District Council. Consequently, the corporation dropped Immingham Dock and Great Coates from its proposal. The remainder of the proposed extensions were subject to a Local Government Board public inquiry in February 1908. The question of public health became a major issue during the inquiry. Grimsby's inadequacies were heavily criticised, especially when compared with Cleethorpes' much better record in building control and sanitation. Not surprisingly, the Local Government Board rejected Grimsby's entire bid.[12]

Privy Boxes

During the inquiry a contrast was made between Cleethorpes' good record in replacing privy boxes with water closets and Grimsby's poor record. In 1904 the borough surveyor said that, of 13,000 houses in Grimsby, 9,000 had privy boxes. The following year the boxes were described as 'disgusting and dangerous' and a committee was appointed to consider the question. The death a year later of Dr Thomas Newby, who had acted as medical officer of health for both Grimsby and Cleethorpes, called forth the press comment that he had been bitterly opposed to the privy box system and at Cleethorpes they were being done away with. Lack of action in Grimsby was due in part to the influence of the property interests of some of the council members. These included George Doughty who said, 'We shall require more than a few medical phrases to convince us that the water-borne system has advantage over the box system.' A newspaper commented that as 'Sir George is interested in privy-boxed property the vigorous attack upon decency, cleanliness, safety and comfort is not surprising.'[13] However, the corporation decided in 1908 to do something about the privy boxes. Even so, a local newspaper foresaw that special interests on the council would create problems: 'Some members of the corporation own property where these abominations exist, and we may expect to hear some special pleading.' Not surprisingly, the corporation made the rather weak-kneed decision that 'as far as possible' privy boxes should be replaced by water closets. But work began and 100 privies were replaced by water closets during one month.[14]

A Storm in a Tankard

Something else that was to cause problems for the corporation was the question of public houses. In general, developers of large estates did not want public houses on their land. They were reckoned to encourage drunkenness, unruly behaviour and immorality. Consequently they diminished the value of property in their neighbourhood. Owners of leasehold estates could debar them by the use of covenants in the leases, such as Heneage's strictly enforced covenant that prohibited the 'trade of licensed victualler or beerhouse keeper'. In those parts of the town nearer to the docks, such as on the freemen's East Marsh, it would have been difficult to prohibit sales of alcohol. There was also the financial consideration for the freemen that public houses paid a much higher annual ground rent than other types of buildings.

In their contrasting approaches neither Heneage nor the freemen had a serious problem with liquor licensing. The corporation was not so lucky. As the end of the 19th century approached, the corporation leases started to expire for the plots that had been leased out in the East Marsh Lots and East Fitty Lots at the beginning of the century. Although the corporation had sold the freeholds of most of the plots early in the century, 75 remained in corporation ownership. The properties comprised two distinct groups: 41 were in the

77   *Flottergate and the* Black Swan *public house (the 'Mucky Duck') in 1969 before their demolition during the redevelopment of the town centre.*

King Edward Street area and 34 were along the north side of Cleethorpe Road either side of the railway level crossing. The properties included four public houses on Cleethorpe Road, namely the *Alexandra Hotel*, the *Exchange Hotel*, the *Victoria Hotel* and the *Sheffield Arms*. Their leases were all due to expire in 1901. The corporation would be then in the happy position of being the outright owner of these buildings and able to extract much larger rents from the premises – and so increase its income. But when was life so simple?

Grimsby had a large body of temperance supporters who were determined that the corporation should let the liquor licences lapse and then close the four public houses. Many supporters of the liquor and brewing interests opposed them, and also those ratepayers who believed that the corporation should seize this opportunity to increase its income and, hopefully, lower the municipal rates. Battle was fully joined in 1901. It was a battle with political overtones. In general the Liberals supported temperance and the Conservatives the liquor trade. The temperance lobby attacked vigorously with large-scale protests and letters cascading on the local press. In response to the onslaught, the council decided to compromise and retain only two licences. The liquor lobby then counter-attacked, citing the financial implications of this decision and the fact that closing two public houses would make no difference to the amount of drunkenness in the town.

Tension ran high at meetings of the council and in July 1901 the *Grimsby News* reported a meeting at which there was a 'volcanic explosion ... and such disgraceful scenes as are a disgrace to our town'. Conflict continued and the licences became a major issue at the local elections in November. There was a record poll and it was stated that nine of those elected as councillors supported keeping all four licences. The battle ended as the new council voted by 26 votes to 18 to retain all the licences and keep the four public houses open. The financial importance of the public houses is shown by the fact that in 1907 they produced a total annual rent of £687, which was one-third of the total rents received from all the corporation's 34 properties on Cleethorpe Road. Still, it was a spirited debate that enlivened the local scene until the froth settled on this local storm in a tankard.[15]

Continuing Growth

In addition to public houses, more services and public buildings were provided as the town continued to grow. By 1905, the gas company had 10,390 consumers. It opened a sales shop in 1904 in Sheepfold Street and a showroom in Victoria Street in 1909. The Osborne Street showroom opened in 1928. The corporation's electricity works in Doughty Road opened in 1901. Hospital provision was improved with the completion of the Springfield Isolation Hospital in 1900. Educational buildings included the Education Office in Eleanor Street (1900), the distinctive Strand Street School with its rooftop playground (1912) and the town's first public library (1901, housed in the old Mechanics' Institute building in Victoria Street). The strength of the police force had grown from four men in 1846 to 65 in 1901 while the corporation's volunteer fire brigade had a complement of 27 men and two fire engines. New entertainment venues included the Palace Theatre (built 1904 and demolished 1979), the Tivoli Variety Theatre (built 1905, destroyed by bombing 1943) and several cinemas. New churches included a replacement (brick-built) All Saints Church (1906), St Paul's Church in Corporation Road (1908, replacing the mission church), Welholme Congregational Church (1908, incorporating the Granville Street mission church that had opened in 1895), Weelsby Road Methodist Church (1909), Watkin Street Roman Catholic Church (1909), St Augustine's Church (1911) and St Luke's Church (opened 1912 and demolished 1969). Brighowgate was graced with two fine buildings by prolific local architect H.C. Scaping: the exuberant Courthouse (1902) contrasting with the classical lines of the Children's Home (1913) – both now with different uses.

78 *Welholme Congregational Church on the corner of Hainton Avenue and Welholme Road. It was completed in 1908 and is seen here soon after its opening.*

79   *The Brighowgate Children's Home. Opened in 1913, it became a Salvation Army Hostel in 1959. It is viewed here in 1963.*

80   *The County Courthouse in Brighowgate, built in 1902. Seen here in 1989.*

81   *Suburban-looking Weelsby Road in the 1930s. Portland Avenue leads off on the extreme right.*

Although outside engineers, architects and contractors were used by the railway company for dock and railway construction, most of the fabric of the town was laid out and designed by local surveyors and architects, including, in addition to Scaping, Joseph Maughan, E.W. Farebrother, W. Wells, J.J. Cresswell and others. The construction of all manner, size and quality of buildings, the making of roads and other construction work was dependent on a plethora of local builders, including Riggall and Hewins (later Hewins and Goodhand), George Doughty, John Brown, Edwin Tyson and many others, along with their numerous workforces.

The End of an Era

With the outbreak of the First World War in 1914, Grimsby came to the end of an era. It had experienced an extraordinary period of physical expansion. Its population had soared from about fifteen hundred in 1801 to about eighty thousand in 1914. John Wesley's 'middling village' was now being referred to as the premier fishing port in the world and the town was also a thriving commercial port. All this had taken place during a period that was marked by one particular characteristic. This was a widely held opposition to 'interference' in local matters by either central or local government. Although those who had forwarded the town were not operating within a truly 'free for all' economy, they certainly had a much freer hand than would apply after the war. The railway company had set the ball rolling and its dynamic chairman claimed to have made the town. Landowners set out and built their estates largely as they wished. The freemen pursued their 'No Surrender' policy and dreamt of ever-increasing dividends. In the centre sat the inadequate municipal corporation struggling to cope with challenges to its authority, both from within and without.

However, the years preceding the First World War showed signs of changes that would bring fresh influences to bear on the town's development when peace returned. On the one hand, some things in the town seemed to belong to past ages, such as the carriers' carts that came into the Bull Ring and Old Market Place every week from 33 local villages.[16] On the other hand, some things belonged to a coming age, such as the newfangled motorised public and private transport, which would help in the creation of residential suburbs and commuter villages. Even the all-important railway was changing. The pioneering MS&LR had become the GCR, which had heavy commitments in other areas, including Immingham.

New ideas on urban planning were coming to the fore. We have seen how Heneage and Grant-Thorold could ignore the needs of the town during their sparring in the late 19th century. Now there was a growing national awareness that more control should be exercised over urban development. Consequently, the Housing and Town Planning Act of 1909 permitted local authorities to draw up town planning schemes. The Grimsby corporation considered the new legislation but took no concrete action yet. Other likely changes were on the cards in the administration of the corporation. William Grange died in office in 1913 and later in the year the borough council appointed its first full-time, non-freeman town clerk. He was J.W. Jackson, who had been deputy town clerk of Salford. Although under the Pastures Act he was obliged to serve as clerk to the enrolled freemen, his wider local government experience and his clear primary full-time responsibility to the corporation augured well for a more modern and professional approach to the corporation's administration.

Fresh ideas on the construction and layout of housing were highlighted in 1905 by the initiative of members of the corporation in visiting, at their own expense, the first garden

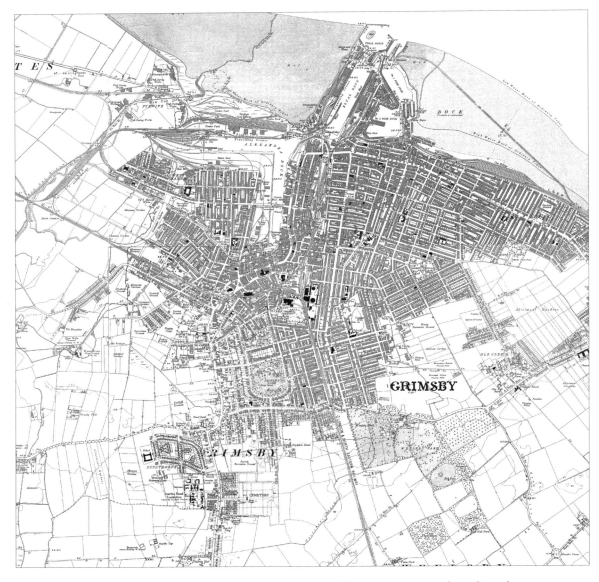

82   *Grimsby, 1933. Building had continued to expand in all directions. Housing now lay to the south of Weelsby Road and the Nunsthorpe council estate lay south of Laceby Road. To the west, building had extended into Little Coates.*

city at Letchworth. On their return, the borough surveyor, by now H.G. Whyatt, reported that the houses had beautiful elevations and cottages were built there for £150. However, they were constructed of temporary materials and would cost £250 if built to comply with local building regulations and byelaws; consequently no action followed.[17] There was also an increasing interest in the building of 'council houses' by local authorities. Several acts of parliament during the later Victorian period gave local authorities limited powers to build working-class houses but the general opinion was that it should be left to private enterprise. In 1909 the Grimsby Independent Labour Party proposed that the corporation should build council houses. The negative response was that the corporation saw no reason why

83   *Grimsby, 1946. The rate of building had slowed down when compared with previous maps – partly because of the Second World War. Most new development had been in the west of the town, including the Haycroft, the Little Field and along Yarborough Road.*

it should become a speculative builder.[18] But even while the First World War was being fought, central government was considering the question of post-war housing for the working class. Accordingly, a guidance manual on the provision of suitable housing was issued to local authorities as the war came to an end. It was influenced by the garden city movement and emphasised the need for houses with better layouts and healthier facilities situated in low-density suburban estates. We shall see how these new ideas came to bear on local housing in the post-war period.

Another sign of change was that the owners of large landed estates were finding that the social and financial advantages of their estates were declining. Consequently, many were now thinking the unthinkable and selling land and investing the proceeds in stocks and shares. These thoughts of selling were given a boost by the Liberal government's intention to impose taxation based on the increasing value of land. As a result, the years 1910-14 saw a flood of major land sales across the country. A local example occurred on 10 July 1914 when the 1,456-acre Manor of Bradley was auctioned. Heneage owned a small area but R.N. Sutton-Nelthorpe of Scawby Hall near Brigg owned most of the land. The sale realised £35,445. The Grimsby corporation spent £2,800 in purchasing 97 acres fronting Bradley Road and Laceby Road for use as a cemetery when the Scartho Road cemetery became full. Instead, the land has been used for the Bradley Recreation Ground. It also paid £1,700 for Bradley and Dash Woods (now simply known as Bradley Woods) for use as public walks and pleasure grounds.[19]

Chapter 12

The Twentieth Century and Beyond

So how did Grimsby fare after its era of spectacular growth? This final chapter will provide an overview of what happened in subsequent decades. Industries and town faced new problems, including the devastating effects of two world wars, but innovative technologies opened up new prospects. The glory days of rapidly increasing population were certainly coming to an end. True, the population grew by more than 10,000 during the 1920s but over half of the increase was due to a large-scale boundary extension in 1928. During the 70 years after 1931, the population stayed fairly static, reaching 96,712 by 1961 and settling at 87,574 in 2001, only a few thousand more than its 1921 population.

World Wars

The two world wars probably had a greater economic effect on Grimsby than on many places. Like other towns, its workforce volunteered or was directed into the war effort and it suffered from air raids. However, the big difference was that in both wars its staple industry was devastated as most of its trawlers were commandeered by the Admiralty for use as minesweepers, patrol boats and anti-submarine craft and manned by fishermen who were enrolled into the Royal Naval Patrol Service. Grimsby became the largest minesweeping base in the country during the Second World War. In each war the remnant of the fishing fleet continued to fish to help maintain the nation's food supplies, with the ever-present danger of enemy attack. Local shipyards were turned over to Admiralty work.[1] The Humber Forts were built during the First World War but did not see active service until the second conflict. War work by women included serving in the armed services, nursing, factory work and taking over jobs previously done by men. Thousands of lives were lost in the armed forces. Many trawlers and their crews were lost to enemy action, whether fishing or on Admiralty duties. In the Second World War the town suffered extensive property damage from air raids in which nearly 200 civilians and civil defence personnel were killed.[2] A well-known war effort in the First World War was the production of Tickler's jam. It was not always appreciated by British troops but presumably helped sustain the fighting spirit of the Grimsby Chums battalion as they put new words to a well-known war song and marched through the town singing:

Oh, Oh, Oh it's a lovely war.
What do we want with eggs and ham,
When we've got Tommy Tickler's jam.[3]

Fishing

After each war, the fishing industry had to pick itself up and start all over again. Following the reduced fishing during the First World War, the traditional fishing grounds were well-stocked and were then subject to over-fishing, followed by depression as fish stocks were depleted. Persistent chronic problems in the industry were blamed on the shortage of dock accommodation, leading to trade being lost to other ports including Hull and Fleetwood. It was hoped that a new dock would bring a revival in trade. Under the 1923 reorganisation of the country's railways, the GCR was absorbed into the London & North Eastern Railway (LNER), which 'did not seem disposed to take an enterprising view of the docks' at Grimsby.[4] It certainly declined to finance the capital cost of a new dock. Accordingly, the corporation took a major step forward and, with some help from a government grant, agreed to finance the undertaking. It would then lease the dock to the LNER for 30 years. Over this period the railway would repay the corporation its outlay and then own the dock outright. The dock was opened on 4 October 1934 and had cost nearly £1.75 million. It had a water area of 35 acres and was named No. 3 Fish Dock. The total water area of the three fish docks was now 64 acres.[5] In lauding the dock's excellent facilities, a local newspaper remarked on the overwhelming importance of the fishing industry to the town. It also emphasised current difficulties in hoping that the new dock would mark a 'definite revival of prosperity and expansion in the fishing trade

84   *Old Market Place and Corn Exchange at 11.15 a.m. during the Second World War. Note the ARP van on the left and the group of soldiers in the centre of the picture.*

85   *Grimsby Docks, showing the Royal Dock, Nos. 1 and 2 Fish Docks and (to the right) part of No. 3 Fish Dock.*

of Grimsby'.[6] Following the depletion of near-water fishing grounds, larger and better-equipped trawlers were built to exploit distant-water grounds. But all was not well: more over-fishing; the perishable nature and varying quality of the product; the variations in supply and demand; the effects of the weather and the extreme privations and dangers of fishing marked an industry with a high degree of uncertainty.

Despite its problems, fishing was still the town's dominant industry after the Second World War. In 1964, British vessels landed 158,545 tons of white fish at the port and the value of all fish landed exceeded £13 million. Ever bigger and better-equipped ships were built and new distant-water grounds were opened up. But this was to be the industry's final flourish and in the mid-1970s it was effectively killed off. The cause was a combination of factors, which included over-fishing and declining fish stocks, competition from foreign fishing fleets, the so-called Cod Wars of 1952-76 during which Iceland increased its coastal fishing limits to 200 miles, the loss of Norwegian and Russian fishing grounds, the European Union's Common Fisheries Policy and the implementation of fishing quotas.[7] Despite this catastrophe, Grimsby continued to be a foremost fish market, dealing overwhelmingly in fish brought overland from other ports. Because of local expertise in the freezing of fish and vegetables the town also developed as a major food freezing and processing centre – promoting itself as Europe's Food Town.[8]

Commercial Docks

The commercial docks were also beset with uncertainty and depression after the First World War. Coal and timber still comprised the bulk of the traffic but trade overall had declined. In 1913 the tonnage of foreign-going shipping arriving in the port was 2.5 million tons; this fell to an annual average of 1.8 million tons by the early 1930s. Coastal shipping had declined from 558,000 tons to 486,000 tons.[9] Following the nationalisation of the railways after the Second World War, the Grimsby and Immingham docks were transferred to the British Transport Commission in 1949 and then to the British Transport Docks Board (BTDB) in 1963. The BTDB initiated a significant increase in capital investment and by the late 1960s the annual average tonnage of foreign-going vessels arriving in the port had increased to nearly six million tons; similarly, the tonnage of coastal vessels had increased to nearly two million tons. A significant development in 1975 was the importation of Volkswagen cars and light commercial vehicles.[10] When the docks were privatised in 1983, Associated British Ports (ABP) took over the Grimsby and Immingham docks and continued to run them as one port. Major investment over the years resulted in the combined port handling more than 55 million metric tonnes of cargo in 2005, making it the UK's largest port by tonnage; most of this was bulk cargo handled at Immingham. However, by then, Grimsby had become the largest vehicle-handling port in northern Britain, dealing with almost 390,000 vehicles in 2005. Grimsby's other trade included timber imports, bulk raw materials, chemicals, steel products, manufactured goods and imports of frozen fish.[11]

86   *The railway port in action. Dockers on the Royal Dock unloading bananas directly into rail wagons.*

87   *Another view of the railway port in action. Timber being unloaded on the Royal Dock in 1958.*

Industrial Diversity

In the 1920s there was concern about the town being too dependent on fishing and the need to attract new industries. One of the reasons given for getting a boundary extension in 1927-8 was the town's shortage of land suitable for industrial development. This concern resurfaced during the Second World War as the corporation planned in advance for the post-war period. It considered how it could widen the town's industrial base and, accordingly, purchased over 200 acres of land on the Humber bank at Pyewipe for industrial expansion. The land's potential was soon realised and by 1949 most of it had been sold to national or international companies. This led to the rapid development of the petro-chemical, pharmaceutical and man-made fibres industries along the Humber bank as far as Immingham and beyond. The corporation also developed land in the town as trading estates for commerce and light industry.[12]

In 1965, a government report commented that the town was no longer dependent on the fishing industry, which employed only 3,500 people as against 22,000 in manufacturing industries, many of which had been established in the 10 years after the war. It went on to say that Grimsby's economic position was much sounder and more broadly based than it had been at any time since 1914, but it remained isolated from the main communications network of the country.[13] This isolation was compounded when the town's direct railway link with London via Louth was eliminated in 1970 and its final direct service to the capital ceased in 1993. However, a vital link with the motorway network was provided in 1983

88   *Motorised transport taking over from rail? Loading lorries from the fish pontoon.*

with the opening of the A180 West Marsh Relief Road from Lock Hill. Several business estates were developed adjacent to the road, including the 'flagship business park' called Europarc, which was first planned for in 1996. At the time of writing it accommodates a diverse range of companies with a total of 2,000 employees.

Land and Landowners

Town expansion 'on the ground' up to 1914 had been largely at the behest of the major landowners, but after 1918 there was a resurgence of the pre-war sales of land by landed magnates. Although the land taxation that had been set out before the First World War was not exacted, post-war owners were faced with higher income tax, death duties,

increased estate running costs, low agricultural rents and the prospect of more 'interference' from central and local government. An avalanche of sales started throughout the country in 1919. Grimsby landowners joined in this spate of selling in 1920, when it was stated that, 'Times had changed, and practically every great landowner in the country had found it necessary ... to sell portions of his estate'. On 17 March 1920, Lord Heneage auctioned 206 acres of his Highfield Farm land, of which the corporation purchased 104 acres. Part of the land that was sold now contains the Scartho Road Swimming Pool, Barrett's Recreation Ground, Wintringham School grounds and the crematorium. On 29 September 217 acres of the Grant-Thorold estate were auctioned, which later accommodated private and council housing, Hardy's Recreation Ground and the King George V Playing Field.[14]

Lord Yarborough held two sales during 1919-20. About one hundred acres were sold to Sir Alec Black, the local trawler magnate. This land comprised the 71-acre Grange Farm and building plots along Bargate and Laceby Road. Yarborough's other sale comprised six business properties in Haven Street, South Dock Street and West Dock Street, which raised a total of £6,420. Yarborough also sold 128 acres to the corporation for the Nunsthorpe estate for £19,200 in 1919-20. This spate of sales included one in nearby Humberston in 1920 when Lord Carrington auctioned his vast Humberston estate of 3,000 acres.[15] Although sales declined after 1921, a major sale of 740 acres took place in 1927 when the Gilbey estate in Little Coates was put up for auction (with the exception of the Gilbey Road built-up area and the Grimsby golf course). The land for sale lay either side of Yarborough Road and Little Coates Road. Not all the land was taken and further auctions were held in 1928 and 1931 to dispose of the unsold 169 acres.[16]

In April 1930, the Pretyman/Tomline family of Riby sold their Ropery Estate along Cleethorpe Road and Orwell Street (between Riby Square and Humber Street) to Charles Lawson of local retailers Lawson & Stockdale. 1935 saw the auction of the extensive Tennyson leasehold estate. It included properties in Grimsby and Cleethorpes that were producing £3,433 annually in ground rents and was purchased for £115,000 by the trustees of the late W.T. Hewitt.[17]

Although not all the land changing hands during this spate of selling can be accurately quantified, more than 1,300 acres were sold from the Heneage, Grant-Thorold, Yarborough, Tennyson, Pretyman/Tomline and Gilbey estates; plus the 3,000 acres of Carrington's Humberston estate and the pre-war sale of 1,456 acres of Sutton-Nelthorpe's Bradley estate. Of all this land the corporation purchased about four hundred acres and the rest went to sitting tenants, local fishing moguls and other entrepreneurs. Cleethorpes council bought 217 acres at the Humberston sale.

Later in the century some landowners withdrew from the town completely. In 1942, Captain Vivian Hewitt sold the Weelsby Old Hall estate, which the late W.T. Hewitt had purchased from Grant-Thorold, to Frederick Parkes (later Sir) of the Boston Deep Sea Fishing Company. The Old Hall was in use as a hospital annexe until incendiary bombs gutted it in 1943. In 1948, Parkes offered the corporation 130 acres of the land as a public park and pleasure ground. This formed the Weelsby Woods park, which was formally opened on 1 May 1952. The corporation purchased about 60 acres of the estate for council houses.[18]

Lord Heneage died in 1922. His brother, sister, three sons and six daughters all died childless. The upshot of this unlikely scenario was that the title died out in 1967 on the death of his youngest son. James Neil Heneage, who was a great-grandson of Heneage's uncle, inherited the estate. By the 1980s most of the family's leasehold houses in Grimsby had been sold to the householders and only 182 remained in Heneage hands. In 1984 these were sold to a property company for a sum in excess of £150,000, thus severing the family's ancient links with the town. The Yarborough family still owned land in the town. When the 7th earl died in 1991 his estate was valued at more than £67 million. Its 28,500 acres included large areas of forest, about 40 farms and holdings in Grimsby.[19]

While private landowners who had helped determine the shape and character of the town were upping sticks and departing, the freemen maintained their position as a significant landowner, but the value of their annual dividend had declined. In the last full year before the Second World War, 1938-9, the 1,716 freemen each received a dividend of £3 18s. 0d. By the 1950s the leases of property in the Freemen Street area were nearing the end of their 99-year term. Accordingly, in October 1951, a meeting of the freemen decided by an overwhelming majority to renew the leases. New leases for 75 years began to be issued in 1953 at much higher ground rents. The old rents had been set nearly a century earlier and were now financially unrealistic. Accordingly, in the year 1953-4 the 1,660 freemen each received a more reasonable dividend of £7 14s. 0d. The number of freemen and their annual dividend continued to fluctuate through the century and in the year 2001-2 the 1,073 enrolled freemen and widows each drew a dividend of £112.56.[20]

Housing

The aftermath of each of the world wars produced severe housing shortages. For instance, after the First World War, at Bradley Hollow on Laceby Road, people were living in tents, vans and 'bungalows' with no sanitation. Similarly, 20 people who worked in Grimsby were living in holiday 'bungalows' (chalets or huts) at Cleethorpes, and were flooded by the tide in 1921. After the war, government subsidies were made available for both council and private house building. A total of 5,572 houses were built by private builders during the 1920s and 1930s but the days of large-scale landed estate development were spent and new building tended to be piecemeal and along major roads. Heneage's land along the People's Park perimeter was belatedly being filled with villas by the end of the 1920s. There was little initial call for the freemen's remaining land in the Haycroft but demand picked up and by 1938 most of their estate had been leased.[21]

The most significant new departure in local housing was the building of council houses. At the behest of central government, the Grimsby corporation was obliged to come up with a post-war housing scheme. This was despite its lack of enthusiasm and the belief of many of its members that houses should be built by private enterprise, not by local authorities. By October 1919 there was an estimated need for 1,500 council houses in the town, subsequently rising to 2,000, but the council proposed building only 304 on four small sites. The government did not favour the scheme and argued that instead of using small parcels of land at high density the corporation should develop a large 'garden city' suburb of 1,200 houses. Accordingly, the council purchased 128 acres on Laceby Road from Lord Yarborough and reluctantly agreed to build 988 houses over three years. Three years later only 138 had been built. In 1923 the council named the new 'garden city' estate 'Nunsthorpe', which still had only 527 houses by 1935. Public buildings on the estate included St Martin's Mission Church (1922, its replacement, St Martin's Church, was consecrated in 1937), the Maternity Home (1927 and 1933), and junior and senior schools (1931). Other council houses were built in Roberts Street (four houses) and the West Marsh (32 houses). The first council house to be occupied was in Armstrong Street, on the West Marsh, on 3 January 1921.[22]

In the 1930s, local authorities were also required to build houses in order to replace slum dwellings and also to alleviate overcrowding. The corporation did not favour either policy and implemented them at such a sedate pace that neither slum clearance nor overcrowding had been solved by the time the Second World War intervened. The corporation built 714 houses during the 1920s and 1930s, despite government pressure to build more. Because of the high cost of the houses and the corresponding level of rents, many of those for whom the houses were built stayed in lower-rented older accommodation. At one time in 1935 about 50 houses on Nunsthorpe were empty and a local newspaper carried the headline 'Exodus from Nunsthorpe'. The corporation later obtained government permission to lower some rents.[23]

After the Second World War, the situation was exacerbated by the loss of houses due to wartime bombing. In addition, the council had to get stuck into the serious problems of slum

89   *Life carried on even in the dark days of the Second World War. Canon Ainslie School May Queen celebrations, 1941 or 1942. The boys and girls in white tops with dark bracing were the maypole dancers.*

90   *As the war drew to a close, Garden Street held its victory celebrations on 8 May 1945.*

clearance and housing the displaced families. A decision had already been made in 1944 to extend the Nunsthorpe estate, 58 acres adjoining the western boundary of the estate being earmarked by the corporation for council housing. In 1946, 234 prefabricated bungalows (prefabs) went up and by 1952 Nunsthorpe had more than 2,000 houses and a population of eight thousand. By 1947 there were 4,000 applicants for council houses and the council's 1,000th post-war house was completed in September of the following year.[24]

A large-scale housing redevelopment programme was carried out during the 1950s and 1960s. Victorian chickens came home to roost as large swathes of the corporation and freemen's poor-quality housing on the East and West Marsh were demolished under slum clearance plans. Other housing was knocked down to make way for the replanning of the town centre. Displaced tenants were rehoused on the Nunsthorpe, Grange, Springfield, Yarborough and Willows estates. A total of 7,201 houses were built in the borough during 1946-60, of which 4,790 were built by the corporation and 2,411 by the private sector.[25]

By 1980, the council had 11,374 dwellings on its books, a third of all homes in the borough. However, under the 1980 Housing Act council sitting tenants were given the right to buy their dwellings. The corporation had started selling houses to tenants at discounted prices in 1968-9 but the 1980 act gave tenants the right to buy their houses at up to 60 per cent below the market value. Not surprisingly, by 1992 about 2,000 houses had been bought, thus seriously reducing the stock of what became known as 'social housing'. Another government policy initiative then debarred councils from any further house building and empowered housing associations to take on new building schemes. The elimination of the corporation as a provider of housing occurred in 2005 when, after a poll of the council's remaining 8,350 tenants, the council's housing stock was transferred to the Shoreline Housing Partnership, a not-for-profit organisation registered with the Housing Corporation as a social landlord.

Public Transport, Commuting and Boundary Extension

Significant changes were also taking place in public transport. In 1921 the corporation obtained the Grimsby Corporation Act, which included powers for it to purchase the town's tram system. The purchase was agreed in 1925 and in the following year the corporation began to replace the trams with trolley buses and an extended motorbus service. Cleethorpes corporation purchased its section of the tram system in 1936, soon discontinued it, and from 18 July 1937 the two councils ran a joint trolley bus service in place of the tram service. The trolley buses were replaced by motorbuses in 1960. The Prince of Wales opened a new and wider Corporation Bridge in 1928.[26]

Improved public and private motor transport continued to encourage development in what were becoming dormitory villages. Scartho, Waltham, New Waltham, Humberston, Great Coates, Healing and Little Coates were all showing increasing signs of new building. Accordingly, the council promoted a parliamentary bill giving it permission to extend its boundaries. It gave two reasons for doing so: firstly, to take in overspill areas and, secondly, to get land where new factories could be encouraged to set up, and so avoid undue reliance on the fishing industry. Initial strong opposition from neighbouring local government bodies was withdrawn when the corporation agreed to take in only 2,604 acres instead of its original bid of well over 3,000 acres. Also, the freemen decided that freemen living

91 *The new Corporation Bridge decorated for its official opening by the Prince of Wales in 1928. Note the stacks of timber in the background, on the sites of the present Fishing Heritage Centre and Sainsbury's supermarket.*

in the added areas would qualify for the annual dividend. So the bill was unopposed and enacted as the Grimsby Corporation Act of 1927.[27] The new acreage was added to the borough on 1 April 1928, mainly from Little Coates, Scartho and Weelsby plus smaller amounts from Bradley and Great Coates. A welcome 5,485 persons were added to the borough's population. The rate of Grimsby's population growth was declining but that of the commuter villages continued to show marked increases. For example, between 1921 and 2001, Humberston's population increased from 461 to 9,941 (including New Waltham) and Waltham's population increased from 978 to 7,036 (including Brigsley and Ashby-cum-Fenby).

Corporation and Freemen

During the century the municipal corporation grew in stature to become a pivotal and enterprising figure in the town's advancement. We have already noted its purchase of the town's tramway system and its subsequent creation of a comprehensive public transport service. Other signs of change include its enterprise in the 1930s in the initial financing of the No. 3 Fish Dock, its initiative in encouraging industrial diversity in the 1940s and more recent times and its ready acceptance after the Second World War of its role as a provider of council housing. It also tried to make changes in its relationship with the freemen. In 1921 it promoted a parliamentary bill that included powers to acquire, by agreement with the freemen, the freemen's estate and schools. The Pastures Committee took the bold step of recommending these measures to a special meeting of the freemen in January 1921. The freemen voted against its recommendation, the committee resigned and a new committee was appointed. The freemen then petitioned the House of Lords against the proposed measures and the corporation withdrew them from the bill. The bill was enacted as the Grimsby Corporation Act of 1921, which, although lacking any measures to do with the freemen, had a wide range of powers for the 'improvement and good government of the borough'.[28]

During 1922-5 there was a drawn-out wrangle as to whether the freemen had the right to free use of the Town Hall for meetings and it was not until after the Second World War that the fraught relationship between the two bodies was resolved. Under its post-war redevelopment and slum clearance plans the corporation needed to purchase part of the freemen's East Marsh. However, this was not legally possible because under the terms of the Pastures Act of 1849 it was regarded as the trustee of the freemen's land. Accordingly, it applied for an act of parliament that would sever its bonds with the freemen. The freemen opposed the act but it was supported by a town poll in January 1949. Known as the Grimsby Corporation Act of 1949, the measure received royal assent on 31 May 1949, a hundred years after the passing of the Pastures Act. Under the new act, the corporation's trusteeship of the freemen's land was transferred to the Official Trustee of Charity Lands. The corporation could now treat the freemen like any other landowner and purchased large areas of the East Marsh, instigating large-scale housing redevelopment there in the 1960s. Also under the act, the town clerk and the borough treasurer would no longer act as clerk and treasurer to the freemen. This change was stated to be 'for the prevention of difficulties in matters affecting both the corporation and the enrolled freemen' – difficulties that had been apparent ever since the situation was set up under the Pastures Act. The corporation retained its one-twentieth share of the freemen's net income and, as already noted, the freemen's schools were closed.[29]

92 *Freeman Street and trolley bus, looking towards Riby Square from a point between Church Street and Kent Street. Trolley buses replaced trams in 1926.*

Buildings and Redevelopment

New buildings and facilities during the century included the Cromwell Road cattle market (1930), Grimsby Hospital extensions and nurses' home (1933), Duncombe Street Methodist Central Hall (1936, replacing the Methodist Chapel of 1868), crematorium (1954), police headquarters in Victoria Street (1957), Scartho Road Swimming Pool (1962), fire brigade headquarters in Peakes Lane (1964), King George V Athletics Stadium (opened in 1964 on King George V playing fields), Hope Street Fishermen's Mission (1967), Central Library (1968), Cleethorpe Road flyover (1968), Victoria Street Law Courts (1969), St Andrew's Church (1969, the old St Andrew's having been demolished in 1962), Riverhead Centre (1973, recreated and reopened in 1990-1 as the Freshney Place shopping mall), Grimsby Leisure Centre (1975), Scartho Road District General Hospital (1983, renamed the Diana, Princess of Wales Hospital in 1999), National Fishing Heritage Centre (1991), and the Grimsby Auditorium (1995). In addition, the corporation carried out a major school building programme after the Second World War.

During the late 1960s and early 1970s the character of Grimsby's town centre was transformed by a contentious redevelopment scheme. The seeds of it were sown in 1937 when the corporation decided to prepare a town-planning scheme for the central built-

93   *Part of the Nunsthorpe council house estate in 1961. Second Avenue (with the Maternity Hospital) is on the extreme left and Sutcliffe Avenue runs across the centre of the picture with the school and school grounds below it. In the distance are the fields of Scartho Top, later turned over to housing.*

up area. Work on the plans ceased on the outbreak of war but, in 1943, while the war was still being waged, the corporation held an exhibition showing its ideas for post-war redevelopment.[30] Most of the ideas did not reach fruition but one that would in the long-term cause severe public misgivings was a proposal to ease congestion by 'removing' the Victorian Corn Exchange and opening up the medieval Bull Ring and the Old Market Place into one common square. This proposal was eventually enlarged into the wholesale demolition of a major part of the medieval heart of the town and its replacement by what was named St James' Square, a shopping precinct called the Riverhead Centre and car parking. It is ironic that, in 1983, while praising this lacklustre redevelopment, the council remarked on the fine legacy of Victorian and Edwardian buildings that the town possessed. It listed over 300 buildings of architectural and historic interest, also creating conservation areas in Old Clee, Scartho, Great Coates and Wellow.[31] The shape and character of the town continued to change as housing spread on to agricultural areas such as the Laceby Acres and Scartho Top developments.

Local Government Reorganisation

Meanwhile, the corporation pursued a policy of applying for more boundary extensions. The policy was aimed at taking in Cleethorpes, Immingham Dock and nearby commuter villages. Attempts were made in 1946 and 1964-5 but were steadfastly resisted by the Cleethorpes corporation, the Lindsey County Council and the Grimsby Rural District Council. The only gain was the incorporation of the Willows and Wybers Wood areas in 1958 and the Great Coates area in 1968. The policy was overtaken by the countrywide reorganisation of local government in 1974. The northern part of Lincolnshire, including Grimsby and Cleethorpes, was incorporated into the new county of Humberside, which also included East Yorkshire. The new county was divided into several new local government districts. Grimsby was one and had to put up with its existing boundary. Cleethorpes was absorbed into a much larger district that included Cleethorpes itself, the major port of Immingham, 19 villages, an extensive area of agricultural land and petro-chemical works on the bank of the Humber. The new local government structure was a two-tier one with functions divided between the Humberside County Council and the districts. Thus Grimsby lost its self-governing county borough status, which it had fought to achieve in 1891.

Both Grimsby and Hull resented their loss of control of local services, while pressure groups campaigned for a return to the historical counties of Lincolnshire and Yorkshire. There was also widespread national dissatisfaction with the new system. Accordingly, in 1992, a Local Government Commission was set up to examine the provision of local government throughout the country. Not surprisingly, the Grimsby Borough Council quickly came out in support of a single unitary or all-purpose authority. This would combine the Grimsby and Cleethorpes districts and would be large enough not to be subject to any county council control. It would also revert to being in the county of Lincolnshire. Cleethorpes councillors were wary of what they regarded as a Grimsby takeover, but reluctantly accepted that it was inevitable. The outcome was that the county of Humberside was abolished and the Grimsby and Cleethorpes districts were merged to form the unitary authority of North East Lincolnshire. The new authority came into being on 1 April 1996 and Grimsby became part of a local government unit whose councillors were responsible for a total population of 157,979 in 2001, of whom 87,574 lived in Grimsby. But even before the new council took office concern was expressed about its inadequate initial funding and subsequent years saw the council struggling to maintain services.

Summary and Conclusion

During the course of this book we have seen how Grimsby has grown physically 'on the ground' and have examined the factors influencing this process. We have concentrated on the era 1800-1914 because this was the town's time of unprecedented dynamic growth. It was growth that took place within a period of minimum regulation, which encouraged local enterprise but had some unwelcome consequences, such as in the area of public health. Regardless of such drawbacks, it was the activity during this period that determined to a great extent how the town would develop later.

94   *Redevelopment on the freemen's East Marsh, April 1965. Albert Street is awaiting its fate and one of the new tower blocks of flats looms in the background.*

The initial factor in the town's development was its natural haven and its location at the mouth of the Humber estuary. This has been both an advantage and a disadvantage. On the one hand, the haven provided a safe and early landfall and a convenient site for settlement, fishing and sea-borne trade. On the other hand, the town suffered because it was sited in 'an extreme nooke of the kingdome' with no good lines of inland communication. In addition, its location away from the Humber's deep-water channel has been to its disadvantage in recent times.

The lack of inland communication was rectified to some extent with the coming of the railway, which supplied an all-important link with a trading hinterland. Thus the railway became the pivotal factor that led to the town's industrial and residential expansion. Influential 'movers and shakers' in railway and dock provision included entrepreneurs in Sheffield and Manchester and landowners in north Lincolnshire. The municipal corporation provided encouragement and, with the freemen, land for lines and stations. Other participants included engineer James Meadows Rendel with his design and construction of the Royal Dock and his enterprising use of Sir William Armstrong's innovative work on hydraulic engineering. Sir Edward Watkin, who took up the challenge to expand the port's trade, followed them.

The location of the Royal Dock and the fish docks had overwhelming effects on the shaping of the town. Firstly, the initial railway lines to the Royal Dock divided the town physically. Secondly, the docks' location determined the whereabouts and quality of the town's housing. Thirdly, their location created two towns within a town. To the north arose the dockland town with its dock industries and a largely working-class population, while to the south was the old town, which maintained a position as the key professional, business and shopping centre, having a mixed population but within walking distance of residential areas for the better off.

Commercial trade with European ports was increasingly important but it was fishing that became the dominant and overriding factor in the expansion of the port and town. Encouraged and financed initially by both the MS&LR and the GNR, its success and growth were also dependent on the enterprise of smack owners (later trawler owners) and other entrepreneurs, and on the skill and hardiness of the fishermen and boys who faced up to the rigours and dangers of fishing. Grimsby's population could not provide the entire workforce needed to construct railways, docks and the housing for the expanding workforce. Neither could the town provide all the boats and crews that the fishing industry demanded. Consequently, another factor to be considered was the influx of workers and their families. These included navvies, railwaymen, fishermen and fishing apprentices, who came to the town from all parts of the British Isles, and without whom the town and port would not have grown and prospered.

But Grimsby's advancement and expansion could not have taken place without the involvement of local large landowners. Tennyson, Yarborough, Heneage, Grant-Thorold, the municipal corporation, the freemen and others all played important roles in the process. It was Tennyson who proposed building the town's haven dock and, supported by Yarborough and the municipal corporation, got parliamentary approval for its construction. The municipal corporation and the freemen set out the town's first modern extension on the East Marsh Lots and East Fitty Lots. Several of the Yarborough family were involved in bringing the railway to the town and the construction of the Royal Dock. After this, the freemen and the corporation developed their respective estates on the East Marsh and West Marsh with extensive swathes of working-class housing. Later still, Heneage and Grant-Thorold transformed the face and shape of the town when they built up their vast urban estates. Landowners were dependent on their agents and surveyors to bring their policies to fruition. In addition, two groups who were involved in the actual building process were architects and builders, to whom full acknowledgement is due, although their role justifies a separate publication and is not one of the themes that this book has set out to explore.

The municipal corporation and the freemen have had a widespread influence on the town's development but their impact has been uneven and volatile. After their enforced separation in 1835, they had an acrimonious relationship that divided the town and worked against the best governance of the borough; this situation was not resolved until well into the 20th century. However, both bodies helped immigration and town growth by turning their land over to building and providing urgently needed working-class housing. Unfortunately, neither paid enough attention to building standards, sanitation and public health, and most of their housing had to be demolished in the next century.

Other pervasive factors were the 19th-century terminating building societies and the widespread use of leasehold tenure. From the viewpoint of rapid town growth, both were beneficial in encouraging building and home ownership. The building societies channelled local savings into providing the necessary capital for building, while leasehold tenure made it financially easier for builders to start work. Leasehold covenants gave the landowners powers to control the quality of building, although the corporation and the freemen failed to make good use of their powers. Even so, the majority of leasehold houses built for the

95   *Grimsby in 1961, showing (on the left) the transformation of the East Marsh Lots into a trading estate. Part of Victoria Street North and Lock Hill are on the extreme left. To the right is the freemen's East Marsh. Freeman Street is on the extreme right running diagonally up the picture. In the distance are docks.*

96 *The freemen's East Marsh in 1961. Freeman Street runs from lower left to upper right with the covered market in the centre. Areas of close-packed courts and back housing can be seen but a start has been made on the corporation's clearance scheme, particularly in the lower right-hand quadrant.*

97 *Grimsby in 1961.*
Although showing only part of
the town, this picture illustrates
much of its history: St James'
Church (right of centre), which
marks its medieval heart; the
railway line (running across
the picture below the church),
which led to its industrial and
residential expansion; the dock
and other industries to the north
and the nearby close-packed
working-class housing. In
contrast, there is the varied and
spacious housing layout to the
south with its gardens and trees.

98   *A final nostalgic view of the basic reason for Grimsby's rapid growth. Little more than a century after the railway came to town, this train from Sheffield makes its way along the old MS&LR line over the Friargate crossing as it approaches Grimsby Town Station c.1955.*

working class in Grimsby during the 19th century were of better quality than the small number of comparable freehold houses.

With the advance of the 20th century, national factors began to have a strong influence on the town's physical development. These included the first stirrings of town planning, the drive for the provision of improved working-class housing and the building of subsidised council housing, to which were added the withdrawal of major landowners from Grimsby. These factors came to the fore after the First World War, which itself was a major setback for the town. But by then the municipal corporation was playing an increasingly positive role in local development. It purchased land for public amenities, provided council housing (admittedly with initial reluctance) and took over and improved public transport. The widespread improvements in public and private transport encouraged the spread of the town's working population into suburbs, overspill areas and nearby villages. This helped the corporation to gain a major extension of the borough's boundary in 1928. The corporation also assisted local industry, including the initial financing of the construction of the No. 3 Fish Dock. The Second World War was another serious check on local advancement but the local authority greeted peace with major plans for building and industrial diversification. These included its initiation of industrial development on the Humber bank and the creation of trading estates in the town. After the traumatic collapse of the fishing industry, the town profited from its expertise in food freezing and processing.

As the 20th century neared its end, outside factors became increasingly more influential. These included the country's membership of the European Union, regional planning and the domination of the area's industry by national and multi-national companies, which were more and more subject to the ups and downs of international trade and finance, with consequent implications for local employment, prosperity and development. Another outside influence was central government's repeated investigation into reorganising local government in the quest for its holy grail, the perfect local government system. Hopefully, the quest ended as the Grimsby corporation's favourite dream came true and the town was merged with Cleethorpes and Immingham in the creation of the unitary authority of North East Lincolnshire in 1996, just in time for the town to gird its loins, ready to face the challenges of another century.

Appendix 1

Grimsby Population and Houses
1801-2001[1]

Year	Population	Houses
1801	1,524	265
1811	2,747	668
1821	3,064	733
1831	4,048	822
1841	3,700	958
1851	8,860	1,676
1861	11,067	2,364
1871	20,244	4,272
1881	28,503	6,245
1891	51,934[2]	11,245[2]
1901	63,138	13,841
1911	74,659	16,243
1921	82,355	16,986
1931	92,458[3]	20,470[3]
1941	No census because of Second World War	
1951	94,557	25,571
1961	96,712	29,702
1971	92,960	31,010[4]
1981	92,596	32,486[4]
1991	90,517	35,427[4]
2001	87,574	36,846[4]

Notes

[1] Sources: Victoria County History of Lincolnshire Vol.II (1906) pp.366-7 and the 10-yearly census volumes. (GCL Local History Library)

[2] The increases in population and houses shown in the 1891 census are due partly to the extension of the borough boundary to take in Clee-with-Weelsby in 1889.

[3] The increases in population and houses shown in the 1931 census are due partly to the extension of the borough boundary to take in Scartho and Little Coates in 1928.

[4] The figures given for houses refer to 'Households' in the 1971, 1981, 1991 and 2001 censuses.

Also note that some census volumes show variations between the original census figures and later revisions.

Appendix 2

Grimsby or Great Grimsby?

Wbat is the correct name of the town that has been the subject of this book? Should it be Grimsby or Great Grimsby? During its long history, the town has been called both, with a variety of spellings. About 12 miles to the south of Grimsby lies its much smaller namesake, the hamlet of Little Grimsby. In the year 1086, Domesday Book referred to both places as Grimesbi. Thirty or so years later in the Lindsey Survey of 1115-18, the hamlet was entered as Parva Grimesbia (Little Grimsby) but the town was again cited as just Grimesbi. In the following century, the town's royal charter of 1201 referred to Grimsby. Later documents emanating from the crown and central government used either Grimsby or the Borough of Grimsby and early church records refer to the parish of Grimsby.

The expanded name appeared on the scene by 1293 with a Latin reference to Magnam Grymesby (Great Grimsby). Records of the 1400s reveal the town being referred to as Magna Grymesby, Grete Grimesby and Gret Grymesby. In 1477 a merchant's will was described as that of 'John Sheryffe of Great Grimsby'. In 1535 the borough court rolls began to use the terms Great Grimsby, Magna Grimsby and Grimsby Magna. These names were also used in other documents and the first parish register of St James' Church referred to Great Grimsby in 1538. Writing in the following century, Gervase Holles referred to the town as both Grimesby and Great Grimesby. The medieval town seal bore the inscription Grimsby but a new one, which was adopted in the mid-1600s, read Grimsby Magna.

The name Great Grimsby does not appear to have been in common use during the succeeding centuries. However, the local Haven Act of 1796 mentions the Town and Port of Great Grimsby and the ensuing century saw a growing use of the fuller name. The town's poll books during the period 1820-68 refer to the Borough of Great Grimsby, the 1827 Enclosure Act cites the Parish of Great Grimsby, government commission reports of 1832 and 1834 refer to the Borough of Great Grimsby and in 1849 George Babb signed himself as Town Clerk of Great Grimsby. Later in the century, official bodies such as the Historical Manuscripts Commission and the Ordnance Survey called the town Great Grimsby. Also, as the town's industry and commerce expanded many of the new firms used Great Grimsby in their names. In 1832 the enlarged Grimsby constituency was called the Parliamentary Borough of Great Grimsby – but in 1918 reverted to simply Grimsby. The use of the fuller name declined in the new century but, in the 1950s, the St James' Church parish magazine was still flying the flag with a Great Grimsby heading on its front cover.

Possibly with a sense that it was time to revive the ancient usage and encourage civic pride, the borough council officially changed the name of the borough to Great Grimsby with effect from 1 January 1979. Consequently, from then until 1995, the council's town guides bore the title Borough of Great Grimsby. In 1996, the Great Grimsby and Cleethorpes boroughs were amalgamated to form the new local authority of North East Lincolnshire.

So what is the current situation? The writer's correspondence with the North East Lincolnshire Council in January 2007 produced the reply that the 1979 official adoption of the title Great Grimsby has never been rescinded and that the correct name of the parliamentary constituency is the Parliamentary Borough of Great Grimsby. Also, central government's Secretary of State for the Environment used the full name when, in 1996, he created the official body known as the Charter Trustees of the Town of Great Grimsby whose duties include custodianship of the town's historic insignia and regalia and the promotion of the 'good name of Great Grimsby'. Consequently, attractive town boundary signs now refer to the Town of Great Grimsby and a council official has suggested to the writer that 'it may be an idea to remind all and sundry of the correct title of Grim's gift to us all' – and who would want to disagree with him? So perhaps now really is the time to put the Great back into Grimsby.

Sources for Appendix 2

Agenda for the Annual Meeting of the Great Grimsby Borough Council on 16th May 1979; Together with a Portrait of the custom, practice and tradition by which the Borough has been known as Great Grimsby. Passim.

Cameron, K., *The Place-names of Lincolnshire: Part Five, the Wapentake of Bradley* (1997), pp.46-7.

Author's correspondence with North East Lincolnshire Council, January 2007.

Foster, C.W. and Longley, T., *The Lincolnshire Domesday and the Lindsey Survey* (1924), paragraphs 3/19; 4/70-1; 14/84; 22/25; 30/14; 36/1; 70/13-14; L9/2,5; L10/4,7.

Historical Manuscripts Commission, *The Manuscripts of Lincoln, Bury St Edmunds and Great Grimsby Corporations* (1895), p.278.

Holles, G., 'Memorials of the Holles Family, 1493-1656', edited by A.C. Wood, *Camden Society, 3rd Series, Vol. LV* (1937), p.229.

Abbreviations

CEF	Clerk to the Enrolled Freemen
ELR	East Lincolnshire Railway
GCL	Grimsby Central Library
GCR	Great Central Railway
GDT	*Grimsby Daily Telegraph*
GET	*Grimsby Evening Telegraph*
GFP	*Grimsby Free Press*
GG&SJR	Great Grimsby & Sheffield Junction Railway
GGG	*Great Grimsby Gazette*
GI	*Grimsby Independent*
GN	*Grimsby News*
GNR	Great Northern Railway
GO	*Grimsby Observer*
GT	*Grimsby Telegraph*
LA	Lincolnshire Archives
LNER	London & North Eastern Railway
LRSM	Lincoln, Rutland & Stamford Mercury
MS&LR	Manchester, Sheffield & Lincolnshire Railway
NA	National Archives, Kew
NELA	North East Lincolnshire Archives
SMR	Sidney Sussex College Muniment Room

References

Chapter 1: An Extreme Nooke of the Kingdome

1. Holles, G., 'Memorials of the Holles Family, 1493-1656', edited by Wood, A.C., *Camden Society, 3rd Series, Vol. LV* (1937), p.230.
2. Weiss, J. (translator), *The Birth of Romance, an anthology: Four 12th-century Anglo-Norman romances* (1992), pp.43-4.
3. Gillett, E., *A History of Grimsby* (1970), p.7; Rigby, S.H., *Medieval Grimsby: Growth and decline* (1993), p.5.
4. Cameron, K., *The Place-names of Lincolnshire: Part Five, the Wapentake of Bradley* (1997), p.75.
5. Weiss, *The Birth of Romance*, pp.xxiii, xxv, xxviii; Gillett, *Grimsby*, pp.6-7; Cameron, *Place-names*, p.48; Rigby, *Medieval Grimsby*, p.5; Byng, J., *The Torrington Diaries: A selection from the tours of the Hon. John Byng between the years 1781 and 1794*, edited by Bruyn Andrews, C., (1954), p.367; *Kelly's Lincolnshire Directory* (1913), p.247.
6. Foster, C.W., and Longley, T., *The Lincolnshire Domesday and the Lindsey Survey* (1924), paragraphs 4/70-1; 30/14; 36/1.
7. Rigby, *Medieval Grimsby*, pp.8, 20; Wise, P.J., 'The Archaeology of the Grimsby-Cleethorpes Area', in *Humber Perspectives: A region through the ages*, edited by Ellis, S., and Crowther, D.R. (1990), p.221.
8. Gillett, *Grimsby*, pp.2, 21.
9. Gillett, *Grimsby*, pp.2, 3.
10. Rigby, *Medieval Grimsby*, pp.8, 44; G. Fox, *The History of Pontefract* (1827), p.15.
11. Rigby, *Medieval Grimsby*, pp.86-8.
12. Rigby, *Medieval Grimsby*, pp.46, 83.
13. Rigby, *Medieval Grimsby*, p.80.
14. Historical Manuscripts Commission, *The Manuscripts of Lincoln, Bury St Edmunds and Great Grimsby Corporations* (1895), pp.107, 283, 286.
15. Rigby, *Medieval Grimsby*, pp.13-15, 53-9.
16. Rigby, *Medieval Grimsby*, pp.9-10, 64-7, 77; Gillett, *Grimsby*, pp.31-2, 36; Rothwell, H. (ed.), *English Historical Documents, Vol.III, 1189-1327* (1975), p.883; Foster, *Lincolnshire Domesday*, p.79.
17. Rigby, *Medieval Grimsby*, pp.69-73.
18. Gillett, E.E., Russell, R.C. and Trevitt, E.H., *The Enclosures of Scartho, 1795-1798 and of Great Grimsby, 1827-1840* (1964), p.1.
19. Thirsk, J., *English Peasant Farming* (1957), pp.65-6.
20. Gillett, *Grimsby*, pp.106, 186-7.

21. Gillett, *Grimsby*, p.106.

22. Rigby, *Medieval Grimsby*, pp.29-30, 127-31; Platts, G., *Land and People in Medieval Lincolnshire* (1985), pp.218-29.

23. Rigby, *Medieval Grimsby*, pp.30-2, 115; Gillett, *Grimsby*, p.21.

24. Rigby, *Medieval Grimsby*, pp.98-9, 104, 119, 138.

25. Rigby, *Medieval Grimsby*, pp.127-31; Gillett, *Grimsby*, p.95.

26. Holles, Memorials of the Holles Family, p.229; Holles, G., *Lincolnshire Church Notes*, edited by Cole, R.E.G., (1911), p.vi.

27. Holles, *Lincolnshire Church Notes*, p.2.

28. Gillett, *Grimsby*, p.141.

29. Greenfield, L., *Grimsby's Freemen, contrasted with the Freemen of other towns* (1950), p.33.

30. Gillett, *Grimsby*, pp.160, 162.

Chapter 2 : New Dock, New Town, 1796-1830s

1. Jackson, G., *Grimsby and the Haven Company, 1796-1846* (1971), p.13; 36 Geo III, c.98, *An Act for Widening, Deepening, Enlarging, Altering, and Improving the Haven of the Town and Port of Great Grimsby, in the County of Lincoln*, 1796.

2. Jackson, *Grimsby*, pp.24, 29.

3. Jackson, *Grimsby*, p.50.

4. Jackson, *Grimsby*, pp.8-9, 17; Crossland, G., and Turner, C., *Great Grimsby: A History of the Commercial Port* (2002), p.18.

5. Gillett, *Grimsby*, p.177.

6. Gillett, *Grimsby*, p.177; Jackson, *Grimsby*, pp.38-9.

7. Jackson, *Grimsby*, pp.39-40; Gillett, *Grimsby*, p.204.

8. Jackson, *Grimsby*, pp.41-2, 49-50.

9. Gillett, *Grimsby*, p.213; Bates, A., *A Gossip about Old Grimsby* (1893), p.12.

10. Dowling, A., 'The Corporate Landowner in Town Development: with particular reference to Grimsby and Cleethorpes, c.1800-c.1900' (PhD thesis, Hull University, 1997), pp.44-5.

11. Royal Commission on Municipal Corporations in England and Wales, *Appendix to the First Report. Parts IV and V. Report on the Borough of Great Grimsby* (1835), pp.2256-7.

12. Royal Commission on Municipal Corporations, p.2250.

13. Gillett, *Grimsby*, p.205.

14. Gillett, *Grimsby*, p.193.

15. Gillett, *Grimsby*, p.151.

16. Byng, *Torrington Diaries*, p.367.

17. Greenfield, *Grimsby's Freemen*, pp.46-7; Royal Commission on Municipal Corporations, p.2251.

18. Gillett, *Grimsby*, p.202.

19. Greenfield, *Grimsby's Freemen*, pp.49-50.

20. NELA, 2/920/1, *Acts and Documents relating to the Borough and Seaport of Great Grimsby, compiled and arranged for private use by Thomas Stephenson, Grimsby*, 1851.

21. NELA, 1/953/8, Municipal Corporation lease to John Watson, 1800; 1/102/14, Mayor's Court Book, 12 November 1799; 17 December 1799.

22. NELA, 2/920/1, *Acts and Documents*.

23. NELA, 1/102/14-16, Mayor's Court Book, 3 December 1805; 10 March 1829; 22 December 1835; 1/110/1, Grimsby Corporation Minutes, 15 March 1836.

24. NELA, 1/102/14, Mayor's Court Book, 1 September 1801.

25. Jackson, *Grimsby*, pp.43-4.

26. GCL, Skelton Papers, 1845, Vol.4, No.82; NELA, 1/110/1, Grimsby Corporation
    Minutes, 26 April 1838.

Chapter 3 : Reform and Divide, 1827-1840

1. GCL, Skelton Papers, 1824, Vol.1, No.54.
2. GCL, Skelton Papers, 1829, Vol.1, No.14; Royal Commission on Municipal Corporations,
    pp.2254-5; GCL, Skelton Papers, 1828, Vol.2, No.135.
3. NELA, 1/102/15, Mayor's Court Book, 31 October 1826.
4. GCL, Skelton Papers, 1827, Vol.1, No.13.
5. Gillett, Grimsby, p.190.
6. 7 & 8 Geo. IV, c.18, *An Act for Dividing, Inclosing and Exonerating from Tithes, Lands in the
    Parish of Great Grimsby, in the County of Lincoln, 1827*; NELA, 1/102/15, Mayor's Court
    Book, 6 February 1827; 1/901/2, Grimsby Enclosure Award, 1840.
7. Royal Commission on Municipal Corporations, p.2254.
8. GCL, Skelton Papers, 1829, Vol.1, No.33; NELA, 1/102/15, Mayor's Court Book, 12
    May 1829.
9. Gillett, *Grimsby*, p.203.
10. Greenfield, *Grimsby's Freemen*, p.50; NELA, 1/102/16, Mayor's Court Book, 17 March
    1831; GCL, *The Poll for the Election of a Burgess to serve in Parliament for the Borough of
    Grimsby taken on Monday, Dec.10th 1832*, p.36.
11. Smellie, K.B., *A History of Local Government* (1968), p.30.
12. Gillett, *Grimsby*, p.212.
13. NELA, 1/102/16, Mayor's Court book, 28 July 1835; Greenfield, *Grimsby's Freemen*, p.60.
14. NELA, 1/110/1, Grimsby Corporation Minutes, 19 August 1839; 5 November 1839; 19
    December 1839; 23 November 1841.
15. Gillett, *Grimsby*, p.212; Greenfield, *Grimsby's Freemen*, p.51.

Chapter 4 : Railway and Conflict, 1835-1849

1. NELA, 1/102/16, Mayor's Court Book, 20 September 1831; Gillett, *Grimsby*, p.213.
2. Dow, G., *Great Central*, Vol.1 (1959), p.85.
3. Dow, *Great Central*, Vol.1, pp.84-5.
4. 9 & 10 Vict. cap. 268, *An Act to Amalgamate the Sheffield, Ashton under Lyne and
    Manchester Railway Company, the Sheffield and Lincolnshire Junction, the Sheffield and
    Lincolnshire Extension and the Great Grimsby and Sheffield Railway Companies, and the
    Grimsby Docks Company, 1846*.
5. Dow, *Great Central*, Vol.1, pp.111, 141; Hodgkins, D., *The Second Railway King: The Life
    and Times of Sir Edward Watkin, 1819-1901* (2002), pp.118-19.
6. NELA, 1/110/1, Grimsby Corporation Minutes, 2 March 1846.
7. GCL, Skelton Papers, 1847, Vol.1, No.1.
8. NELA, 1/110/1, Grimsby Corporation Minutes, 15 February 1847; 20 November 1847;
    GCL, Skelton Papers, 1847, Vol.1, No.1.
9. GCL. Skelton Papers, 1845, No.103; 1846, Vol.2, No.142.
10. GCL, Skelton Papers, 1847, Vol.2, No.148.
11. LRSM, 17 October 1847, p.2.
12. LRSM, 5 November 1847, p.2; GCL, Skelton Papers, 1847, No.170; NELA, 1/110/1,
    Grimsby Corporation Minutes, 11 August 1848.

13. GCL, Skelton Papers, 1848, Vol.2, No.131.
14. GCL, Skelton Papers, 1848, Vol.2, No.163.
15. 12 & 13 Vict. c.16, *Grimsby Pastures Act 1849*, sections 3-7, 10-11, 34-7, 39, 66; GCL, Skelton Papers, 1854, Vol.1, No.48a.
16. Greenfield, *Grimsby's Freemen*, p.62.
17. NELA, 1/110/1, Grimsby Corporation Minutes, 7 February 1842; 7 August 1843.
18. *GN*, 11 September 1903, p.6.
19. *LRSM*, 5 February 1847, p.3; R. Lincoln, *The Rise of Grimsby*, Vol.2 (1913), pp.261-2.
20. Lincoln, *Grimsby*, Vol.1, p.370.
21. NELA, 1/110/1-2, Grimsby Corporation Minutes, 11 August 1848; 12 March 1849.
22. NELA, 1/102/15, Mayor's Court book, 28 June 1825; 5 July 1825; *Grimsby Pastures Act 1849*, section 72; Lincoln, *Grimsby*, Vol.1, p.292.
23. *GGG*, 16 October 1857 p.2; 24 December 1857 p.2; *GFP*, 8 June 1860 p.3; *GN*, 10 November 1882 p.8; *GO*, 26 February 1879 p.2.
24. *GN*, 10 November 1882, p.8.
25. *Grimsby Pastures Act 1849*, section 21.
26. *LRSM*, 26 October 1849, p.2.
27. GCL, Skelton Papers, 1849, Vol.2, No.222.
28. *GN*, 17 April 1896, p.5; *GO*, 22 April 1896, p.2.
29. *GO*, 19 August 1891, p.2.
30. *GN*, 12 September 1899, pp.4, 6.
31. Dowling, Corporate Landowner, p.136.
32. *GFP*, 11 January 1861 p.2; 6 May 1864, p.2; *GO*, 29 November 1871, p.4.
33. *GO*, 20 June 1877, p.2.
34. *GFP*, 27 July 1860, p.2; GCL, Skelton Papers, 1861, Vol.2, No.152.

Chapter 5 : Railway Port, 1849-1880s

1.   NA, RAIL 1110/304, Report of Directors of MS&LR to the Proprietors and First General Meeting, 17 February 1847.
2.   Bates, *Old Grimsby*, p.6.
3.   Jackson, G., *The History and Archaeology of Ports* (1983), p.90.
4.   GCL, Skelton Papers, 1849, No.62.
5.   Dow, *Great Central*, Vol.1, p.125.
6.   Dow, *Great Central*, Vol.1, p.125.
7.   Dow, *Great Central*, Vol.1, p.125.
8.   Dow, *Great Central*, Vol.1, pp.173, 175; Jackson, *Ports*, p.90; Lee, S. (ed.), *Dictionary of National Biography* (1896), pp.10-12; Crossland and Turner, *Great Grimsby*, pp.30, 39-40.
9.   NA, RAIL 463/1, MSL&R shareholders' meeting, 1850.
10. Dow, *Great Central*, Vol.1, pp.151-3; Crossland and Turner, *Great Grimsby*, pp.31-2.
11. Dow, *Great Central*, Vol.1, pp.163, 175; Crossland and Turner, *Great Grimsby*, pp.45, 46, 53, 57, 59.
12. Lee, S. (ed.), *Dictionary of National Biography, 1901-11* (1912), pp.601-3.
13. Dow, *Great Central*, Vol.1, p.160.
14. GCL, Tidal Harbours Commission, *Minutes of Evidence taken before Capt.Washington, R.N., at Great Grimsby on the 24th October 1845, as to the Past and Present State of the Port* (1845), pp.6, 11.
15. Dow, *Great Central*, Vol.1, p.176.

16. *Tesseyman's Directory and Hand Book to the Port of Grimsby* (1852), p.42.

17. NA, RAIL 1110/304, Reports & Accounts of Railway Companies, 1846-68.

18. *Gait's Grimsby and Cleethorpes Directory 1871*, p.34; *Gait's Post Office Directory of Grimsby and Cleethorpes 1880*, p.xvi.

19. Boswell, D., *Sea Fishing Apprentices of Grimsby* (1974), pp.40-1.

20. Alward, G.L., *The Sea Fisheries of Great Britain and Ireland* (1932), p.22; Crossland and Turner, *Great Grimsby*, pp.37, 71-4.

21. Dow, *Great Central*, Vol.2 (1962), pp.162-3, 167; Crossland and Turner, *Great Grimsby*, p.47.

22. Dow, *Great Central*, Vol.1, p.176; Vol.2, pp.149, 155.

23. GGG, 24 April 1857, p.2.

24. *Gait's directory 1871*, p.29.

25. GO, 3 November 1875, p.2.

26. Hodgkins, *Second Railway King*, p.126; NA, RAIL 1007/348, Papers on Sir Edward Watkin.

27. Folkestone Library, unpaged clipping from the *Hythe and Sandgate Echo*, 22 October 1881.

28. GN, 19 April 1901, p.3.

29. Ranger, W., *Report to the General Board of Health on a preliminary inquiry into the sewerage, drainage, and supply of water, and the sanitary condition of the inhabitants of the Borough of Grimsby in the county of Lincoln* (1850), p.3.

30. GCL, Skelton Papers, 1849, Vol.2, No.225; NELA, 1/110/2, Grimsby Corporation Minutes, 9 November 1849.

31. Ranger, *Report to the General Board of Health*, pp.5-7.

32. Ranger, *Report to the General Board of Health*, pp.50-3.

33. NELA, 1/110/2, Grimsby Corporation Minutes, 20 October 1852.

34. GCL, Skelton Papers, 1852, Vol.2, No.154c; NELA, 1/110/2, Grimsby Corporation Minutes, 17 February 1853.

35. 16 & 17 Vict. Sess. 1852-3, *Great Grimsby Improvement Act 1853*.

36. Ranger, *Report to the General Board of Health*, p.5.

37. *Great Grimsby Improvement Act 1853*, Schedule A; NELA, 1/110/2, Grimsby Corporation Minutes, 5 April 1855.

38. *GT* 20 April 2006, p.18, 'Bygones' column; Newbery, J.A., 'Public Health in Grimsby from 1800 to c.1872' (MA Thesis, Hull University, 1976), p.142.

39. Newbery, 'Public Health', pp.ix, 122-6.

40. *Tesseyman's Directory 1852*, pp.17-18, 43.

41. *White's History, Gazetteer and Directory of Lincolnshire 1856*, pp.577-8.

Chapter 6 : *Building the East Marsh, 1840s-1870s*

1. LRSM, 11 June 1847, p.2.

2. GCL, Census Enumerators' Returns, Grimsby, 1851.

3. Dowling, Corporate Landowner, pp.61-2; Ranger, *Report to the General Board of Health*, p.51; Newbery, Public Health, map 5.

4. Ranger, *Report to the General Board of Health*, pp.18, 21, 23, 25-6, 35-6; NELA, 1/860/31/2, Letter [I.N?] Simpson to Earl of Yarborough, 21 July 1853; GO, 6 March 1872, p.1.

5. GCL, Census Enumerators' Returns, Grimsby, 1851 and 1871; Ranger, *Report to the General Board of Health*, pp.23, 25; GO, 22 March 1876, p.3.

6.   *GO*, 10 January 1872, p.3.
7.   Dowling, Corporate Landowner, p.67.
8.   *Grimsby Pastures Act 1849*, p.3, sections 37, 39; GCL, Skelton Papers, 1849, Vol.2, No.225; 1854, Vol.2, No.95.
9.   Lincoln, *Grimsby*, Vol.1, p.293; GGG, 13 March 1857, p.2.
10. Lincoln, Grimsby, Vol.1, p.293; GGG, 13 March 1857, p.2; GCL, Skelton Papers, 1850, Vol.1, No.82.
11. GGG, 26 May 1857, p.2; 3 July 1857, p.3; 12 June 1857, p.3; 19 June 1857, p.2; 3 July 1857, p.3.
12. GGG, 3 July 1857, p.3.
13. GO, 24 August 1892, p.2; GGG, 19 Sept 1857, p.3; GCL, Skelton Papers, 1858, Vol.1, No.77a; NELA, 1/922/3, Plan of East Marsh, 1857.
14. GGG, 18 September 1857, p.3; GCL, Skelton Papers, 1858, Vol.1, No.77a.
15. GGG, 25 September 1857, p.2.
16. GGG, 24 December 1857, p.2; NELA, 1/110/3, Grimsby Corporation Minutes, 26 May 1866.
17. GI, 27 May 1859, p.2.
18. GI, 11 June 1858, p.2; GGG, 26 February 1858, p.2.
19. GI, 11 June 1858, p.2; GGG, 17 September 1858, p.2; 8 October 1858, p.2; M. Gerrish, 'Special Industrial Migration in 19th-Century Britain: a case study of the port of Grimsby, 1841-61' (PhD thesis, Hull University, 1992), pp.206-7.
20. GI, 10 September 1858, p.2.
21. GI, 24 September 1858, p.2; 15 October 1858, p.2; 19 November 1858, p.3; GGG, 22 October 1858, p.3; NELA, 473/1/1, Pastures Committee Minutes, 13 April 1861.
22. GI, 26 November 1858, p.4; 3 December 1858, p.2; 25 March 1859, p.2.
23. GO, 10 July 1872, p.4; Dowling, Corporate Landowner, p.147.
24. NELA, 473/1/1, Pastures Committee Minutes, 5 July 1860; Lincoln, Grimsby, Vol.1, p.365.
25. GO, 26 June 1872, p.4; NELA, 473/3/15, 25, Freemen's Rentals 1871, 1881; GO, 10 July 1872, p.4.
26. GO, 19 May 1875, p.2.
27. GO, 29 January 1873, p.4.
28. *Gait's Directory 1871*, p.21.
29. NELA, 1/110/3, Grimsby Corporation Minutes, 18 December 1865; *Grimsby Pastures Act 1849*, section 48; Lincoln, *Grimsby*, Vol.1, pp.296, 323.
30. GO, 5 June 1872, p.4; NELA, 473/1/1, Pastures Committee Minutes, 9 October 1876; 18 February 1878; 27 May 1864; 17 April 1879.
31. GO, 23 June 1886, p.2; 1 July 1896, p.2; 31 March 1897, p.2; GN, 4 June 1901, p.8; 22 October 1901, p.8.
32. CEF, Pastures Committee lease to Henry Stephens, 9 January 1860.
33. NELA, 473/1/1, Pastures Committee Minutes, 8 May 1863; 3 December 1863; 14 July 1864; 24 October 1864; 12 June 1865; 3 July 1872; GO, 5 March 1873, p.1; Ordnance Survey, 25-inch map, *Lincolnshire (Parts of Lindsey)*, sheet XXII 7, 1890.
34. *Gait's Directory 1871*, p.31.
35. GO, 20 August 1873, p.4.
36. GO, 6 June 1877, p.4.
37. GO, 11 June 1879, p.3.
38. GO, 5 June 1872, p.4.
39. GO, 4 June 1884, p.2; 3 June 1885, p.2; 10 June 1885, p.2.
40. GO, 6 June 1888, p.3.

41. *GFP*, 16 November 1860, p.2.
42. NELA, 473/1/1, Pastures Committee Annual Report for 1868-9, in Pastures Committee Minutes, 26 May 1869; Pastures Committee Minutes, 9 October 1876; Pastures Committee Rent Roll 1871; *GO*, 20 December 1876, p.2; Dowling, Corporate Landowner, p.147.
43. *Gait's Directory 1871*, p.8.
44. *GO*, 15 October 1873, p.1.
45. *Gait's Directory 1871*, p.24.
46. CEF, Pastures Committee Annual Report, 1871-72.

Chapter 7: Building the West Marsh, 1870s

1.   Post Office Directory of Grimsby and Cleethorpes 1890, pp.xi-xii, 123-230; *GN*, 10 August 1894, p.2.
2.   Humberside County Council, Index to the Freemen's Roll Book of Grimsby, 1780-1980 (1994), *passim.*
3.   Olney, R.J., *Lincolnshire Politics, 1832-85* (1973), p.5; *GN*, 8 November 1901, p.5.
4.   *GN*, 26 October 1894, p.5; 2 November 1894, p.8; White's Directory of Grimsby 1895, pp.8-9.
5.   *GO*, 16 February 1876; 30 August 1884, p.3; *GN*, 16 November 1892, p.2.
6.   NELA, 1/110/4, Grimsby Corporation Minutes, 8 March 1875; 1/110/5, Grimsby Corporation Minutes, 9 November 1875; 1/110/6, Grimsby Corporation Minutes, 3 August 1886; *GO*, 8 October 1873, p.4.
7.   Gillett, *Grimsby*, p.237.
8.   32 & 33 Vict. c.10, *Grimsby Improvement Act, 1869*; *GO*, 14 August 1872, p.4; 10 July 1872, p.4; 14 August 1872, p.4.
9.   *Gait's Directory 1871*, pp.29-30.
10. *GO*, 12 March 1873, p.4; 9 April 1873, p.4; 19 March 1873, p.4; NELA, 1/110/4, Grimsby Corporation Minutes, 2 October 1873; 13 October 1873.
11. NELA, 1/110/4, Grimsby Corporation Minutes, 28 November 1873.
12. *GO*, 3 December 1873, p.4; NELA, 1/110/4, Grimsby Corporation Minutes, 5 December 1873.
13. *GO*, 7 January 1874, p.2; NELA, 1/110/4, Grimsby Corporation Minutes, 9 February 1874; 13 March 1874; 18 March 1874; 7 October 1874.
14. *GO*, 12 March 1873, p.4; NELA, 1/110/4-5, Grimsby Corporation Minutes, 13 March 1874; 18 March 1874; 7 October 1874; 20 December 1875; 3 October 1877.
15. *GO*, 18 February 1874; 11 December 1872, p.4; 1 January 1873, p.4.
16. NELA, 1/110/4, Grimsby Corporation Minutes, 5 February 1873.
17. *GO*, 12 February 1873, p.4.
18. *GN*, 9 August 1895, p.6; NELA, 1/110/4, Grimsby Corporation Minutes, 16 May 1873; 1/110/7, Grimsby Corporation Minutes, 17 April 1893; *GO*, 25 March 1896, p.2.
19. *GO*, 20 August 1873, p.4.
20. *GO*, 5 February 1873, p.4; 17 March 1873, p.4; 8 October 187,3 p.4; 1 September 1875, p.3.
21. *GO*, 15 October 1873, p.4.
22. NELA, 2/514/2, Grimsby Corporation Rental 1873-4; 2/332/2/1, Grimsby Urban Sanitary Authority, General District Rate, 1883.
23. Dowling, Corporate Landowner, p.79.
24. *GO*, 8 September 1875, p.2; 1 September 1875, p.3; 4 July 1877, p.2; 18 August 1875, p.2; 6 October 1875, p.2; 20 April 1881, p.3.

25. NELA, 1/110/1, Grimsby Corporation Minutes, 23 November 1841; 1/110/2-4, Grimsby Corporation Minutes, 2 August 1852; 27 July 1855; 16 October 1863; 23 August 1867; 1 February 1869.
26. GN, 17 January 1908, p.5; NELA, 1/110/8, Grimsby Corporation Minutes, 14 March 1899.
27. GO, 24 August 1892, p.2; NELA, 1/110/5, Grimsby Corporation Minutes, 2 October 1876; 16 November 1876; GO, 6 March 1878, p.3; LA, 2 HEN 5/1/57; NELA, 1/110/5-6, Grimsby Corporation Minutes, 15 August 1884; GO, 3 September 1884, p.3; 17 September 1884, p.3; 4 September 1884; 28 November 1884; 3 December 1884, p.2.
28. GO, 7 March 1877, p.3; 20 March 1889, p.2.
29. GO, 5 April 1876, p.2; 10 January 1877, p.3; 6 March 1878, p.3; 27 March 1878, p.2; 27 March 1878, p.2.
30. GCL, The Tennyson Estate sale catalogue, 1935.
31. GFP, 7 June 1861, p.2.

Chapter 8 : Building Clee and Weelsby, 1860s-1880s

1. Dover Castle Henry VIII exhibition, June 2003.
2. LA, 2HEN 5/1/1, letter, 23 June 1860, William Bartholomew to John Wintringham.
3. LA, 2HEN 5/1/9, letter, 25 March 1867, William Bartholomew to John Wintringham; 5/4/20, correspondence, January 1877.
4. LA, 2HEN 5/1/70 letter, 4 October 1879, Joseph Maughan to John Wintringham.
5. GO, 14 August 1872, p.4.
6. GO, 12 March 1873, p.4.
7. LA, 2HEN 1/1/31; 2HEN 5/4/117, correspondence, January 1877.
8. LA, 2HEN, 4/2/1/39, letter, January 1877, Joseph Maughan to John Wintringham; 4/1/1/24, Heneage Grimsby estate draft accounts 1877; 5/4/123, correspondence 1877.
9. GO, 16 April 1873, p.4.
10. LA, 2HEN, 5/4/120, letter, 16 August 1877, Edward Heneage to John Wintringham.
11. Gait's Directory 1880, pp.xxx-xxxi.
12. LA, 2HEN 4/1/1/38, printed letter, April 1884, Edward Heneage to John Wintringham.
13. LA, 2HEN 5/1/58, letter 24 January 1870, Edward Heneage to John Wintringham; 5/4/68, correspondence, 1876; 4/1/1/38, printed letter, April 1884, Edward Heneage to John Wintringham.
14. Dowling, A., 'The Urban Development of the Weelsby Estate at Grimsby of Edward Heneage, 1870-1890' (BA dissertation, Hull University, 1986), pp.56-61.
15. GO, 30 October 1872, p.4.
16. GO, 19 February 1873, p.1; 12 March 1873, p.4; NELA, 2/331/3/2, Clee Parish Rate Book, November 1886.
17. GO, 14 October 1885, p.2; 21 October 1885, p.2; 30 October 1889, p.3.
18. GCL, Census Enumerators' Returns, 1871 and 1881.
19. GO, 7 April 1881, p.2; 16 November 1881, p.4.
20. Report from the Select Committee on Town Holdings together with the proceedings of the committee, minutes of evidence and appendix (1887) (260) Vol.XIII, p.234.
21. NELA, 1/110/4, Grimsby Corporation Minutes, 16 May 1873; 4 August 1873; 8 March 1875; GN, 14 December 1883, p.6.
22. NELA, 1/110/7, 1/110/9, Grimsby Corporation Minutes, 7 April 1911; 5 May 1911; 12 January 1912; 12 April 1912; 27 February 1894; 7 August 1894.
23. GO, 24 March 1880, p.2; LA, 2HEN 5/11/5, letter, 21 January 1884, Edward Heneage to John Wintringham; GN, 27 July 1883, p.4; 5 October 1883, p.5.

24. GO, 26 March 1884, p.4; LA, 2HEN 4/1/1/38, printed letter, April 1884, Edward
     Heneage to John Wintringham; 5/11/35-39, letters, April 1884, Edward Heneage to John
     Wintringham; 5/12/28, letter, 30 March 1885, Leasehold Enfranchisement Association to
     John Wintringham.
25. GO, 12 February 1896, p.2.
26. GO, 26 March 1884, p.2.
27. Parliamentary Papers, 1888, XXII (313) *Town Holdings*, questions 8316, 8388, 8452-3.
28. GO, 7 May 1873, p.4; 21 May 1873, p.4.
29. GO, 26 March 1884, p.2.
30. NELA, 1/111/1, County Borough of Grimsby Printed Agenda Papers, 9 June 1892; GO, 3
     August 1892, p.3; 24 August 1892, p.2.
31. GO, 9 May 1877, p.3; 9 December 1877, p.2; GN, 13 May 1877, p.3; NELA, 1/971/3,
     Clee-with-Weelsby Local Board of Health Bye-laws 1880.
32. NELA, 1/971/1/2, Clee-with Weelsby Local Board Minutes, 18 April 1888; 21 March
     1888; 1/971/1/3, 30 January 1889.
33. Dowling, Urban Development of the Weelsby Estate, p.7.

Chapter 9 : Expansion and Independence, 1880s-1891

1.   NELA, 1/110/6, Grimsby Corporation Minutes, 3 December 1886.
2.   GO, 8 December 1886, p.3.
3.   GN, 18 March 1887, p.5.
4.   GO, 11 May 1887, p.3; 18 May 1887, p.2; 25 May 1887, p.3; 24 August 1887, p.2; GN, 19
     August 1887, p.8.
5.   GO, 8 August 1888, p.3.
6.   Drury, E., *The Old Clee Story*, p.38.
7.   GO, 28 January 1889, p.3.
8.   GO, 3 April 1889, p.2.
9.   GO, 30 January 1889, p.2; 27 February 1889, p.3; 52 & 53 Victoria, Session 1889, *Grimsby
     Extension and Improvement Act, 1889*; County Borough Celebrations in the People's Park,
     Thursday April 9th 1891, Official Programme.
10. GO, 15 April 1891, p.3.

Chapter 10: Controversial Times, 1890s

1.   GN, 3 May 1895 p.6; 2 August 1895 p.5; 9 August 1895, p.6.
2.   GCL, The Tennyson Estate sale catalogue, 1935; GN, 28 October 1904, p.5.
3.   NELA, 1/110/7, Grimsby Corporation Minutes, 26 June 1893; 31 March 1894; GO, 14
     February 1894, p.2; 12 September 1894, p.2; 19 September 1894, p.2; GN, 10 June 1904,
     p.5; 8 July 1904.
4.   NELA, 1/110/7, Grimsby Corporation Minutes, 9 June 1893; 1/110/8-9, 11 June 1897; 3
     August 1897; 1 August 1899; 26 August 1898; 30 June 1899; 4 August 1903; 5 December
     1911; 12 April 1912.
5.   NELA, 1/110/4, Grimsby Corporation Minutes, 1 May 1870.
6.   NELA, 1/110/8-9, Grimsby Corporation Minutes, 8 January 1897; 7 July 1905; 5 January
     1906; GN, 3 October 1905, p.6; GO, 9 September 1891, p.2; GCL, County Borough of
     Grimsby, *Incorporation Scheme, Local Government Board Inquiry, Proceedings* (1908), p.424.
7.   NA, RAIL 463/13, MS&LR Proceedings of the Board of Directors, 30 May 1873; 27 June 1873.

8. GN, 13 October 1905, p.5.
9. GN, 10 April 1906, p.6; 1 June 1906, p.4; 22 June 1906, p.5; 20 July 1906, p.4; 28 September 1906, p.4; 1 May 1908, p.6.
10. House of Commons. *Select Committee on Railway Bills*, Session 1891, p.376.
11. LA, 2HEN 5/4/120, letter 16 August 1877, Edward Heneage to John Wintringham.
12. LA, 2HEN 4/2/18/5, letter July 1887, Edward Heneage to I.D. Good.
13. NELA, 1/150/1, Grimsby Corporation Highways Committee Minute Book, 4 April 1892; GO, 8 June 1892, p.2.
14. LA, 2HEN 4/2/18/93-4, memorandum, July 1892, Borough Surveyor to Grimsby Corporation Highways Committee.
15. LA, 2HEN 5/19/44, 47, letters, August 1892, Edward Heneage to John Wintringham.
16. LA, 2HEN 4/2/18/93-94, memoranda, July 1892, Borough Surveyor to Grimsby Corporation Highways Committee.
17. LA, 2HEN 5/46/156, correspondence, June-July 1897.
18. LA, 2HEN 5/46/156, correspondence, June-July 1897; 4/2/17, Heneage Estate Book, 1877-1925.
19. GO, 15 November 1871, p.4.
20. GFP, 28 March 1862, p.2; GO, 22 October 1890, p.2; 24 December 1890, p.3.
21. GO, 23 January 1889, p.3.
22. GN, 27 October 1899, pp.6-7.
23. GN, 23 June 1903, p.6.
24. NELA, 473/1/1, Pastures Committee Minutes, 20 May 1870; 20 April 1875; 1/110/4, Grimsby Corporation Minutes, 5 December 1873; GO, 9 June 1875, p.2; 3 August 1892, p.3; GN, 5 May 1882, p.6; 22 March 1895, p.4; 2 April 1901, p.6; 4 April 1901, p.6.
25. NELA, 1/110/8, Grimsby Corporation Minutes, 1 June 1903; GN, 8 May 1903, p.5; 2 June 1903, pp.6, 8; 5 June 1903, p.3; 19 June 1903, pp.5-6; 27 November 1903, p.6; 1 January 1904, p.6; 7 June 1904, p.6.
26. GN, 6 June 1905, p.6; 8 March 1907, p.2; 12 & 13 Geo.6 chapter X, Grimsby Corporation Act, 1949, p.3, section 11.
27. GFP, 7 June 1861 p.2; NELA, 473/1/1, Pastures Committee Minutes, 5 April 1871; 1/110/4, Grimsby Corporation Minutes 10 April 1871; 20 October 1871; 8 December 1871; GO, 7 August 1872, p.4; 25 September 1872, p.4; 20 August 1873, p.1.
28. GO, 9 June 1880, p.2; 4 June 1884, p.2; GN, 20 January 1882, p.6; 5 May 1882, p.5; NELA, 1/110/5, Grimsby Corporation Minutes, 16 January 1882; 473/1/1, Pastures Committee Minutes, 19 May 1882.
29. GO, 4 June 1884, p.2.
30. GN, 2 June 1903, p.6.
31. GN, 19 June 1903, p.6; 31 July 1903, p.6; 4 September 1903, p.6.
32. GN, 7 June 1904, p.6.
33. GN, 10 June 1904, p.4.
34. GN, 11 April 1905, p.5; 4 August 1905, p.3; NELA, 1/110/9, Grimsby Corporation Minutes, 1 August 1905.
35. GO, 15 November 1893, p.3; 22 November 1893, pp.2, 4; 6 December 1893, p.2.
36. GO, 12 May 1897, p.3; 4 August 1897, p.2; 27 October 1897, p.3.

Chapter 11 : *Star of the East Coast? 1900-1914*

1. Lincoln, *Grimsby*, Vol. 2, p.435.

2. Alward, *Sea Fisheries*, pp.252, 255; *Kelly's Lincolnshire Directory 1913*, p.247.

3. *Kelly's Lincolnshire Directory 1900*, p.232; *Kelly's Lincolnshire Directory 1913*, p.247; NELA, 1/110/8, Grimsby Corporation Minutes, 9 March 1900; 6 June 1900; *GN*, 29 June 1900, p.4; 30 July 1900, p.7; 7 December 1900, p.7.

4. *GN*, 2 February 1904, p.4; 6 May 1904, p.5; LA, 2 HEN 5/29/3/17; 2 HEN 5/29/28/43.

5. Price, J.H., *The Tramways of Grimsby, Immingham and Cleethorpes* (n.d.), pp.59, 60, 67.

6. *GT*, 25 July 2006, p.16.

7. *GN*, 14 June 1904, p.6.

8. NELA, 473/3/56, Pastures Committee Rent Roll, 1914.

9. NELA, 1/110/9, Grimsby Corporation Minutes, 24 September 1913.

10. NELA, 1/50/1, Grimsby Corporation Highways Committee Minutes, 2 February 1914; 8 June 1914; 26 August 1914.

11. Price, *Tramways of Grimsby*, pp.17, 30.

12. GCL, County Borough of Grimsby, Incorporation Scheme, 1908, *passim*; *GN*, 10 April 1908 pp.5-6; 16 April 1908 pp.3, 5-6.

13. *GN*, 26 April 1904, pp.6-7; 21 August 1906, p.5; 20 November 1908, p.5.

14. *GN*, 12 June 1908, p.5; 11 August 1908, p.4.

15. Dowling, Corporate Landowner, pp.113-19.

16. *Kelly's Lincolnshire Directory 1913*, p.256.

17. *GN*, 13 October 1905, p.2.

18. Hartley, O.A., 'Housing Policy in Four Lincolnshire towns, 1919-1959' (PhD thesis, Oxford University, 1969), p.100.

19. *GN*, 14 July 1914, p.5; *GDT*, 11 July 1914, p.6; NELA, 1/110/10, Grimsby Corporation Minutes, 31 July 1914; 9 November 1914; 8 January 1915.

Chapter 12 : Twentieth Century and Beyond

1. Crossland and Turner, *Great Grimsby*, pp.74, 83-4; *GT*, 13 April 2006, p.21.

2. Smith, M., *Blitz on Grimsby* (1983), pp.1-2, 31-5.

3. Dowling, A., (ed.), *Egging Back O' Doig's* (1995), p.53.

4. *GET*, 4 October 1934, p.1; 5 October 1934, p.4; *GN*, 3 June 1927.

5. *GET*, 4 October 1934, pp.1, 10 and Dock Opening Day Supplement, p.viii.

6. *GET*, 4 October 1934, p.4.

7. Ekberg, C., *Grimsby Fish: the Story of the Port and the Decline and Fall of the Deep Water Industry* (1984), pp.82-3, 101-2.

8. *Great Grimsby Town Guide* (1994-5?), p.21; *Introducing Humberside* (1987-8?), p.32; ABP, *Grimsby and Immingham Handbook* (2006-7), p.42.

9. Jackson, *Grimsby*, p.167.

10. Crossland and Turner, *Great Grimsby*, pp.3, 93; Jackson, *Ports*, p.167; *GT*, 22 September 2006, p.20, '30 Years Ago' column.

11. *GT*, 25 September 2006, p.15, reprinted from *GET*, 25 September 1973; Crossland and Turner, *Great Grimsby*, pp.3, 94, 99; ABP, *Ports Handbook* (2005), pp.29-32; ABP, *Grimsby and Immingham Handbook* (2006-7), p.38.

12. County Borough of Grimsby, *Visit of His Royal Highness the Duke of Edinburgh, Wednesday July 13th, 1949, Souvenir Programme*; Ward, F.W., 'A Town of Dynamic Growth and Great Opportunities' in *Borough of Grimsby Official Guide* (1983), pp.40-4.

13. Local Government Commission for England. *Report and Proposals for the Lincolnshire and East Anglia General Review Area* (1965), p.5.

14. GCL, Highfield Farm sale catalogue, 1920; Grant-Thorold Estate sale catalogue, 1920.

15. GCL, Grange Estate sale catalogues, 1931, 1946; Warehouses, Wharfage Rights and Offices sale catalogue, 1920; Humberston Estate sale catalogue, 1920.
16. GCL. Gilbey Estate sale catalogues, 1927, 1928, 1931.
17. GDT, 30 April 1930, p.7; GCL, Tennyson Estate sale catalogue, 1935; GN, 28 June 1935, p.5.
18. Drury, Old Clee, pp.49-50, 70, 79.
19. GET, 28 June 1984; 15 October 1991, p.1; 16 October 1991, p.1.
20. GET, 9 October 1951; 4 May 1953; 8 June 1954; Letter dated 3 October 2002 to the author from the Clerk to the Enrolled Freemen.
21. Gillett, Grimsby, p.294; Dowling, A., Humberston Fitties, the story of a Lincolnshire Plotland (2001), pp.121-2; Hartley, Housing Policy, p.146; CEF, Pastures Committee Annual Report, 1937-8.
22. Hartley, Housing Policy, pp.103-5; GET Bygones, 18 September 1993, pp.20-21; GT, 11 October 2004, p.13.
23. Hartley, Housing Policy, pp. 114, 117, 118, 121, 146; Gerrish, M., Old Nunsthorpe: The 'Garden City' Dream (1998), p.28.
24. Hartley, Housing Policy, pp.121, 125-6; GET Bygones, 18 September 1993, pp.20-21; GT, 25 January 2005, p.18.
25. Hartley, Housing Policy, p.146.
26. 11 & 12 Geo.5, Ch.l xxvi, Grimsby Corporation Act, 1921; Price, Tramways of Grimsby, pp.36-7, 44, 100.
27. GT, 17 December 1926; 3 May 1927; 5 May 1927; 9 May 1927; GN, 7 January 1927; 3 June 1927.
28. CEF, Minute Book of the Annual Meetings of the Enrolled Freemen, 20 January, 14 February, 28 February, 6 June 1921; Grimsby Corporation Act, 1921, p.1.
29. Grimsby Corporation Act, 1949; GET, 8 January 1949.
30. County Borough of Grimsby, Grimsby Tomorrow, leaflet (1943).
31. Borough of Grimsby Official Guide (1983), pp.21-3.

Sources and Bibliography

Clerk to the Enrolled Freemen, Grange & Wintringham, St Mary's Chambers, West St
 Mary's Gate, Grimsby, DN31 1LD
Grimsby Central Library, Local History Collection, Town Hall Square, Grimsby, DN31
 1HG
Lincolnshire Archives, St Rumbold Street, Lincoln, LN2 5AB
Muniment Room, Sidney Sussex College, Cambridge, CB2 3HU
National Archives, Kew, Surrey, TW9 4DU
North East Lincolnshire Archives Office, Town Hall Square, Grimsby, DN31 1HX

Books

Alward, G.L., *The Sea Fisheries of Great Britain and Ireland* (1932)
Ambler, R.W., 'The Historical Development of Grimsby and Cleethorpes', in *Humber
 Perspectives: A region through the ages*, edited by S. Ellis and D.R. Crowther (1990)
Baines, W. (translator), *The Lay of Havelock the Dane* (1980)
Barber, R. (ed.), *Myths and Legends of the British Isles* (1999)
Bates, A., *A Gossip about Old Grimsby* (1893)
Beresford, M., *New Towns of the Middle Ages* (1967)
Boswell, D., *Sea Fishing Apprentices of Grimsby* (1974)
Byng, J., *The Torrington Diaries: A selection from the tours of the Hon. John Byng between the
 years 1781 and 1794*, edited by C. Bruyn Andrews (1954)
Cameron, K., *The Place-names of Lincolnshire: Part Five, the Wapentake of Bradley* (1997)
Chapman, P., *Grimsby: The Story of the World's Greatest Fishing Port* (2002)
Crossland, G. and Turner, C., *Great Grimsby: A History of the Commercial Port* (2002)
Dictionary of National Biography, edited by S. Lee (1896)
Dow, G., *Great Central*, 3 vols. (1959, 1962, 1965)
Dowling, A., *Cleethorpes: The Creation of a Seaside Resort* (2005)
Dowling, A. (ed.), *Egging Back O'Doig's: A Glossary of Words and Expressions used in
 Grimsby, Cleethorpes and District* (1995)
Dowling, A., *Humberston Fitties, the story of a Lincolnshire Plotland* (2001)
Drury, E., *The Old Clee Story* (n.d.)

Ekberg, C., *Grimsby Fish: The Story of the Port and the Decline and Fall of the Deep Water Industry* (1984)

Foster, C.W. and Longley, T., *The Lincolnshire Domesday and the Lindsey Survey* (1924)

Fox, G., *The History of Pontefract* (1827)

Gerrish, M., *Old Nunsthorpe: The 'Garden City' Dream* (1998)

Gillett, E., *A History of Grimsby* (1970)

Gillett, E.E., Russell, R.C. and Trevitt, E.H., *The Enclosures of Scartho, 1795-1798 and of Great Grimsby, 1827-1840* (1964)

Greenfield, L., *Grimsby's Freemen, contrasted with the Freemen of other towns* (1950)

Historical Manuscripts Commission, *The Manuscripts of Lincoln, Bury St Edmunds and Great Grimsby Corporations* (1895)

Hodgkins, D., *The Second Railway King: The Life and Times of Sir Edward Watkin, 1819-1901* (2002)

Holles, G., *Lincolnshire Church Notes*, edited by R.E.G. Cole (1911)

Humberside County Council, *Index to the Freemen's Roll Book of Grimsby, 1780-1980* (1994)

Jackson, G., *Grimsby and the Haven Company, 1796-1846* (1971)

Jackson, G., *The History and Archaeology of Ports* (1983)

Lincoln, R., *The Rise of Grimsby*, 2 vols. (1913)

Loughlin, N. and Miller, K., *A Survey of Archaeological Sites in Humberside* (1979)

Mills, D.R. (ed.), *Twentieth Century Lincolnshire* (1989)

Olney, R.J., *Lincolnshire Politics, 1832-85* (1973)

Platts, G., *Land and People in Medieval Lincolnshire* (1985)

Price, J.H., *The Tramways of Grimsby, Immingham and Cleethorpes* (n.d.)

Ranger, W., *Report to the General Board of Health on a preliminary inquiry into the sewerage, drainage, and supply of water, and the sanitary condition of the inhabitants of the Borough of Grimsby in the county of Lincoln* (1850)

Rigby, S.H., *Medieval Grimsby: Growth and decline* (1993)

Rothwell, H. (ed.), *English Historical Documents, Vol.III, 1189-1327* (1975)

Smellie, K.B., *A History of Local Government* (1968)

Smith, M., *Blitz on Grimsby* (1983)

Thirsk, J., *English Peasant Farming* (1957)

Weiss, Judith (translator), *The Birth of Romance, an anthology: Four 12th-century Anglo-Norman romances* (1992)

Wise, P.J., 'The Archaeology of the Grimsby-Cleethorpes Area', in *Humber Perspectives: A region through the ages*, edited by S. Ellis and D.R. Crowther (1990), pp.213-26

Theses, Articles and Other Sources

County Borough of Grimsby, *Incorporation Scheme 1908, Local Government Board Inquiry, Proceedings* (1908)

Dowling, A., 'The Corporate Landowner in Town Development: with particular reference to Grimsby and Cleethorpes, c.1800-c.1900' (PhD thesis, Hull University, 1997)

Dowling, A., 'The Urban Development of the Weelsby Estate at Grimsby of Edward Heneage, 1870-1890'. (BA dissertation, Hull University, 1986)

Gerrish, M., 'Special Industrial Migration in 19th-Century Britain: a case study of the port of Grimsby, 1841-61' (PhD thesis, Hull University, 1992)

Gillett, E., 'Grimsby and the Haven Company, 1787-1825', in *The Lincolnshire Historian*, Vol.1, 1947-53, pp.359-74

Hartley, O.A., 'Housing Policy in Four Lincolnshire towns, 1919-1959' (PhD thesis, Oxford University, 1969)

Holles, G., 'Memorials of the Holles Family, 1493-1656', edited by A.C. Wood, *Camden Society, 3rd Series, Vol. LV*, (1937)

Local Government Commission for England. *Report and Proposals for the Lincolnshire and East Anglia General Review Area* (1965)

Newbery, J.A., 'Public Health in Grimsby from 1800 to c.1872' (MA Thesis, Hull University, 1976)

Royal Commission on Municipal Corporations in England and Wales, *Appendix to the First Report. Parts IV and V. Report on the Borough of Great Grimsby* (1835)

Tidal Harbours Commission. *Minutes of Evidence taken before Capt.Washington, R.N., at Great Grimsby on the 24th October 1845, as to the Past and Present State of the Port.* (1845)

Ward, F.W., 'A Town of Dynamic Growth and Great Opportunities' in *Borough of Grimsby Official Guide* (1983)

Index